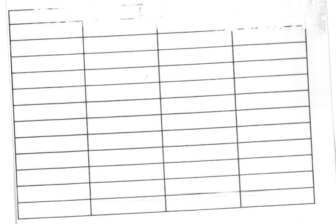

AS TIME GOES BY

MEMOIRS
OF A
WRITER

Time Goes By

BY
HOWARD
KOCH

HARCOURT BRACE JOVANOVICH · NEW YORK AND LONDON

B
K

Copyright © 1979 by Howard Koch

Requests for permission to make copies of
any part of the work should be mailed to:
Permissions, Harcourt Brace Jovanovich, Inc.
757 Third Avenue, New York, N.Y. 10017

Printed in the United States of America

Library of Congress Cataloging in Publication Data
Koch, Howard.
As time goes by.
1. Koch, Howard—Biography. 2. Screen
writers—United States—Biography.
I. Title.
PS3521.O25Z463   812'.5'2 [B]   78–22260
ISBN 0–15–109769–0

First edition
B C D E

FOR ANNE

FOREWORD

One summer, while fishing on the Rogue River in Oregon, my companions and I came upon a solitary prospector panning for gold, a lingering vestige of the Forty-niners. Tons of sand and gravel must have drained through his sieve before a few bright nuggets were winnowed—a meager living wrested from an indifferent stream. But how can we assess their true value without weighing the pleasure of the quest and the wild beauty of this still-primitive country? Like the prospector, I feel the urge to sift through the past for whatever gold I can find. As for the rest, let the river carry it away.

INTRODUCTION

by John Houseman

One afternoon almost forty years ago, I was sitting in what was humorously known as the executive office of the Mercury Theatre at 41st Street and Broadway when the phone rang and the woman in the box office reported there was someone on his way up to see me. It was a long and complicated climb to the second balcony to what had formerly been the electrician's booth—a narrow, airless room with two large holes in the wall through which arc lights had been aimed at the singers and dancers who had once made the Comedy Theatre one of New York's most distinguished musical houses. They served now as spy holes through which, with growing anguish, I could observe the awful excavations that my partner, Orson Welles, was perpetrating in our expensive stage floor in preparation for *Danton's Death*, the first offering of our second Mercury Repertory season.

When my visitor appeared, he turned out to be a tall, rather shy young man. He was armed with a letter from our principal backer, to whom he had been recommended by the wife of the governor of New York State—Mrs. Herbert Lehman, whose son he had tutored and who had taken a personal interest in his fledgling career. A Columbia Law School graduate, he had rashly opened a law office in Hartsdale but found the money quarrels of his small practice boring; one day he walked out of his office, his eyes on Broadway. Within five years he had had three plays produced, none running long enough to earn a living. Did we have a job for him, a writing job?

He was not a total stranger, as it happened. One of his plays, *The Lonely Man*, had been done by the Federal Theatre in Chicago with a young, unknown actor named John Huston in the leading part. (Typically, it concerned a young Lincoln and his fate in the contemporary world.) I had read it and liked it. And in the forty minutes that we talked, I found its author pleasant, serious, and literate. Since he was willing to work on a salary within the confines of our tight budget, I judged him to be eminently eligible for employment by the Mercury.

In fact, he could not have chosen a better time to climb those stairs. In the summer of 1938, following our first triumphant repertory season, Orson Welles (who had become something of a radio star with "The Shadow") was offered a show of his own on the Columbia network, to be known as "First Person Singular," which he would produce, direct, and narrate, and in which he would play the leading role in stories of his own choosing. He asked me to work with him in the series as editor-writer and co-producer.

Our first show was to be *Treasure Island*, followed closely by Bram Stoker's *Dracula*. At the last moment we reversed the order and opened with a script of *Dracula* which Orson and I had scrawled and pasted together in one seventeen-hour session in Reuben's Restaurant (which boasted that it never closed) between the hours of 6:00 P.M. and noon of the following day.

During the next two months we broadcast a play each week. They included *A Tale of Two Cities, 39 Steps,* short stories by Saki and Sherwood Anderson, *The Count of Monte Cristo,* Drinkwater's *Abraham Lincoln, The Affairs of Anatol,* and *Julius Caesar.*

Mostly because of Orson's charismatic radio presence, the show became a success—so much so that the Columbia network decided to extend it into the fall season with a second series of thirteen. Our name was changed to "Mercury Theatre on the Air" and our time moved to Sunday evening, when we competed with Edgar Bergen and his dummy. The renewal coincided with our preparations for our second Mercury Repertory season, so that between the theatre and the radio show we were now working twenty hours a day.

In desperation we decided to add two new figures to our staff: Paul Stewart came in as associate producer, and I engaged this new writer, Howard Koch. His starting salary was seventy-five dollars, for which he was expected to turn out sixty or more pages of script a week plus the numerous rewrites demanded by Welles and myself. According to Howard, we had "exacting standards" and "considered sleep a luxury" that we denied ourselves and our staff. To aid and guide him in his unfamiliar work, I loaned Howard my ash-blond secretary, an attractive, tireless girl-of-all-work from Smith. He never returned her.

Howard's first assignment for the Mercury was to dramatize *Hell on Ice,* an Arctic epic based on the journals of the ill-fated De Jong expedition to the North Pole. He did so well with this, followed by Booth Tarkington's *Seventeen,* that his weekly stipend was raised to one hundred twenty-five dollars.

For our next show we decided the time had come for a bit of science fiction. We considered Shiel's *Purple Cloud,* then settled on H. G. Wells's *War of the Worlds,* which Howard was to dramatize as a contemporary occurrence in news bulletin form— Orson's idea. Howard objected that the story, as Orson wanted it, meant practically an original play—and he had only six days to write it. He tried to switch us to another property, but by then we were committed.

The panic of October 30, 1938, has been described from many angles by many people. At 9:05 P.M. we believed ourselves to be mass murderers; next day we made the front page of every paper in America and were relieved to learn that there had been no deaths—only one broken arm and several dubious miscarriages. During the next few days we were grilled, then ostracized amid rumors of expulsion from the network. But the following week we signed a contract with Campbell's Soups, went "commercial," and became the "Campbell Playhouse" at a huge increase in our collective emoluments. Koch benefited from this bonanza to the tune of an additional fifty dollars a week. Three months later he departed for Hollywood, where he spent the next twelve years.

There is something of Candide in Howard: his experiences in Hollywood bring to mind the adventures of Voltaire's innocent in the land of Eldorado. Like Candide, Koch finds himself—sincere, trusting, optimistic—moving in continuous wonder from one crisis to another. Unlike him, he emerges with flying colors. Time after time success is thrust on him. For his first Hollywood assignment this modest, mild intellectual is ordered to fashion a vehicle for the swashbuckling Errol Flynn. He studies naval history, Elizabethan politics, and the geography of the Spanish Main and comes up with *The Sea Hawk*—a winner! This is followed by a drama of tropical adultery, Maugham's "The Letter," to which he finds it necessary to add an element of expiation—another winner!

Next this earnest pacifist is set to writing a screenplay based on the lethal exploits of America's number one hero of the First World War—a red-neck marksman by the name of Alvin York. Koch objects that he is the wrong man for the job: he is not interested in shooting—turkeys or Germans. The studio is adamant. Koch perseveres. His pivotal scene becomes York's inner struggle to reconcile his religion with his patriotic duty. The commandment "Thou shalt not kill" was in direct conflict with his participation in an endeavor whose purpose was to kill. To dramatize this subjective process, he and York find a solution in Christ's words, "Render unto Caesar what is Caesar's and unto God what is God's." (Koch observes wryly that "this solution worked well enough at the time and under the circumstances, but, from today's perspective, it seems less convincing. If you render unto the Caesars, past and present, what they demand of us, God comes out on the short end.") Sergeant York, as played by Gary Cooper, was the biggest box-office success of the year. Eighteen months later came *Casablanca* and, later still, my production of *Letter from an Unknown Woman,* directed by Max Ophuls.

Unlike Candide, Howard Koch's optimism proved to be fully justified. In five years he had moved from an unlikely start—student, teacher, lawyer—to recognition as one of the most successful and highly regarded screenwriters in the film business. He had worked with such formidable Hollywood figures as Flynn, Cooper, Michael Curtiz, Huston, Bette Davis, William Wyler, Howard Hawks, Humphrey Bogart, the Warner brothers, Samuel Goldwyn, and many others, and he had come through these associations with his integrity untarnished and his pride intact. He would be needing both in the years ahead, for he was about to enter the dark period of the Hollywood witch-hunts. Yet even here Koch's story takes on strange and special turns. His experience with the film *Mission to Moscow* is a grotesque example of the sort of thing that went on during that incredible era.

Weary from three years of uninterrupted work, Howard had reluctantly declined to write the screenplay when the assignment was first offered him in the summer of 1942. The Warner brothers, Harry and Jack, insisted on his doing it. They assured him that he was uniquely qualified to undertake a patriotic project which, they revealed, was dear to the heart of the president of the United States. Five years later, Jack Warner denounced him as a Red to the inquisitors of the House Un-American Activities Committee, citing his work on that pro-Soviet film as evidence of his Communist sympathies.

Koch went to Washington as one of the Hollywood eighteen (nineteen including Brecht) but not as one of the Hollywood Ten. There was a technical but significant difference—membership in the Communist party. Although many of his friends were members, Howard was too independent to join any political party. But his name was on the letterhead of countless organizations formed out of concern for social justice at home and peace abroad, organizations such as the Hollywood Writers Mobilization (of which he was chairman and I vice-chairman); the Committee for the Arts, Sciences and Professions (HICASP); and, later, the California Arts, Sciences and Professions Council (ASP). As a result Howard spent some time on the Gray List— which meant that offers were still coming to him but in diminishing numbers. His final transition to the blacklist (which Howard describes with characteristic tolerance) is positively Voltairian in its tragic absurdity.

Deprived of their livelihood at home, he, Anne, his wife, and their five-year-old son found themselves with the rest of the political refugees in Europe. Ripped off by a fly-by-night producer in Rome and Paris, he was later able to work in England under an assumed name. By the time he was "rehabilitated" and returned to this country, the film industry had undergone drastic changes; he was never able to recapture the position he had held in Hollywood in the forties. I doubt if he wanted to.

Undefeated and undaunted, he continues to create and, like Candide, to cultivate his garden, which is located up the Hudson from mine, in Woodstock, New York. Year after year he turns out books, film scripts, and plays, which, being on serious and often controversial subjects, he often has difficulty getting produced. Yet he has never lost his courage or his faith in the perfectibility of man. In the face of so much personal evidence to the contrary, he believes in the coming of what he calls the "new people" who will help to make this the "best of all possible worlds."

During our long friendship I have followed the twists and turns of his extraordinary career (Howard says he has lived four lives) which he has faithfully set down in the following pages. When he criticizes aspects of our present society, he does so, again like Candide, in the light of its more humane potential. Nor does he spare himself. He makes no claim to be one of the "new people," but merely their advocate and recorder.

AS TIME GOES BY

THE PANIC BROADCAST

Astronomy tells us that when we observe a distant object, a planet or a star, the image we are viewing is an old one because its light started out long ago. We never merely look out into space, but also back into time. All the images in our telescope are not what *is* but what *was*. In a cosmic sense all things coexist somewhere at any given moment.

However, on a human scale we think of time going by and being irretrievably lost, leaving a part of us somewhere in its wake. But we carry the past with us, everything we have said or done or experienced. In *Casablanca*, for instance, Rick tries hard to shake off his past only to find it still clings to him; the decision he makes at the end of the film has really been made years before under other circumstances.

Looking back at my "time going by," I seem to have lived four lives, five behind the proverbial cat—and who knows what's ahead? My early years were a protracted adolescence, a period of trial and error, during which I was searching for something but not certain what I was looking for. In the course of my explorative twenties I tried religion, I tried teaching, I tried law, I tried affairs, I even tried marriage. Not ready to commit myself fully to any of them, I failed in all of them. However, no failure left me bankrupt either in money or in hope. I simply moved on to something else. A close friend of my youth coined the term *grassing*, which meant to us living day to day and, with some help from our parents, better than our circumstances warranted. Like the medieval theologians who believed the vast sidereal universe revolved around this small planet, I assumed that the world revolved around me. I was mistaken.

At some point the world, so benign to the young in heart, begins to administer some cautionary blows. Bruises occur and the seeds of a neurosis are planted. Perhaps the saving grace in my case was a growing sense that something important was missing in my egocentric life, some integrating force to bind together the neurotic fragments into a whole person. Possibly to compensate for what was lacking in reality, I felt a compulsion to express myself in fiction, to re-create subjectively a world more as I would like it to be, but before I had gained the necessary craft or experience. So I started writing, at first as a dilettante, an amateur, writing as I pleased when I pleased. Then one autumn day, my few royalties from a play used up, I walked into the production office of the Mercury Theatre. Although I didn't know it at the time, this was the beginning of many changes and the prelude to my participation in one of the strangest events in recent history.

The thirtieth of October, 1938, a year before the outbreak of World War II, will be remembered as that extraordinary night when the submerged anxieties of tens of thousands of Americans surfaced in a flood of terror that swept the country. Between eight o'clock Eastern Standard Time and dawn of the next day, men, women, and children in scores of towns and cities across the nation were in panic from objects that had no existence except in their imaginations.

Without knowing more about me than that I had written a stage play which he liked, John Houseman had taken the chance of hiring an unknown to write the Mercury's weekly radio plays. It was an experience, lasting six months, I would not have missed, nor would I want to go through it again. Each week by rehearsal time I was responsible for about sixty pages of script dramatizing some literary work, usually a novel or short story, assigned to me by Orson or Houseman, both of whom had pretty exacting standards. They considered sleep a luxury that, for the most part, they denied themselves as well as their staff. From early morning until late at night my pencil sped and, as energies dwindled, crawled over the yellow pages of my pad to be transcribed and preedited by a young college-girl-of-all-work, Anne Taylor, who somehow managed to read my scrawl and correct my errors. Each batch of twenty or so pages would be rushed over to Welles and Houseman for their criticisms and suggestions. Then came the revisions, until the deadline Sunday noon when Orson took over rehearsals from his assistant and worked his particular magic. For my part in all this I received the lordly sum of seventy-five dollars a week. Only later did I realize the fringe benefits of training and discipline were worth many times my salary. I had finally lost my amateur standing, at least as a writer.

For my third assignment a novella was handed me—H. G. Wells's *War of the Worlds*—with instructions from Orson to dramatize it in the form of news bulletins and first-person narration. Reading the story, which was set in England and written in a different narrative style, I realized I could use very little but the author's idea of a Martian invasion and his description of their appearance and their machines. In short, I was being asked to write an almost entirely original play in six days. I called

Houseman, pleading to have the assignment changed to another subject. He talked to Orson and called back. The answer was a firm "no." It was Orson's favorite project.

On Monday, my one day off, I made a quick trip up the Hudson to visit my family. On the way back it occurred to me I needed a map to establish the location of the first Martian arrivals. I drove into a gas station and, since I was on Route 9W where it goes through a part of New Jersey, the attendant gave me a map of that state.

Back in New York starting to work, I spread out the map, closed my eyes, and put down the pencil point. It happened to fall on Grovers Mill. I liked the sound; it had an authentic ring. Also, it was near Princeton where I could logically bring in the observatory and the astronomer, Professor Pierson, who became a leading character in the drama, played by Orson. Up to then hardly anyone had ever heard of this small hamlet surrounded by farmland; overnight the name of Grovers Mill was heard around the world.

The six days before the broadcast were a nightmare of scenes written and rewritten, pages speeding back and forth to the studio, with that Sunday deadline staring me in the face. Once the Martians had landed, I deployed the opposing forces over an ever-widening area, making moves and countermoves between the invaders and defenders. After a while I found myself enjoying the destruction I was wreaking like a drunken general. After demolishing the Columbia Broadcasting Building, perhaps a subconscious wish fulfillment, I ended the holocaust with one lonely ham radio voice, "Isn't there anyone on the air? Isn't there anyone . . . ?"

By that time it seems that only the hardiest souls, or those who knew it was a play, were still listening. People were fleeing blindly in every direction on foot and in all kinds of vehicles. The scene in Newark, as it was described to me, was one of complete chaos, hundreds of cars racing down streets, disregarding traffic lights to the bafflement of policemen. People in the Riverside Drive area reported to the bewildered police the sighting of Martians in their gigantic machines poised on the Jersey Palisades before wading the Hudson to take possession of New York City.

Years later I was writing a book on the event and was researching happenings in the Grovers Mill area on the night of the broadcast. Most of those who lived there at the time were willing to share their experiences with me. From that perspective they could look back with wry humor even on their misadventures. Not, however, the owner of the Wilson Farm. Reporters and photographers had turned the Wilmarth Farm, as it was called in my play, into the Wilson Farm so that they could photograph an actual place for the news media. The word spread and people came from miles around to see the spot where the first Martian had landed. Hundreds of cars trampled Mr. Wilson's crops. Understandably, he was not amused.

On the other hand, a former fire chief of the neighboring town of Cranbury, whom I shall call Mr. Mathews, enjoyed reminiscing and he found us a willing audience. Mr. Mathews looked like a woodsman, his flesh dropping hound-dog fashion as though it had outgrown his massive frame. Two gold teeth shone like headlights from his grizzled but amiable face. As he recalled the events of that October night, he shook his head in disbelief. Calls kept coming in reporting fires in the woods set off by the Martian heat rays. As a result he spent most of the night chasing fires that had never been lit. In the course of covering the countryside in answer to these false alarms, he had an opportunity to witness what was going on in the area—in his words, "a wild night." Farmers armed with shotguns roamed the countryside looking for Martians. One of the men took a potshot at the windmill in Grovers Mill, mistaking it for a Martian machine, and blew off one of its blades. Later over a hundred New Jersey state troopers were dispatched to the area to calm the populace and disarm these volunteer defenders "before somebody got hurt."

One of the incidents, harrowing at the time but humorous in retrospect, was the experience of a middle-aged couple living in

Cranbury which Mr. Mathews related with a chuckle. Glued to the radio in terror as they listened to the broadcast, the wife had one last wish: to see her parents in Pennsylvania before the end came. The husband jumped into the driver's seat of their car without opening the garage door. When his wife screamed a warning, he paid no attention, gunning the motor and driving right through the door with a splintering crash, yelling back at his wife, "We won't be needing it anymore."

The rest of the story may be apocryphal but Mr. Mathews swears it is true. A half-hour and thirty miles later came the announcement over the car radio that it was only a play. The husband turned the car around and drove home. Coming into his driveway and seeing the smashed garage door, he became so enraged his foot slipped off the brake and fell heavily on the gas pedal. The car plunged through the open garage into the back wall, shattering it to pieces. Instead of a garage, they had an instant carport.

By the end of the broadcast the CBS station switchboard was so deluged by incoming calls that it could no longer function. I recall one story told me by the woman supervising the girls who answered information calls. The company was instituting a new policy of giving the customers more courteous service. Walking down the row of switchboards, my informant heard one of the girls say in a very polite tone, "I'm sorry, we don't have that information here." The supervisor stopped to compliment her. "That was nicely spoken. What did the party ask?" The girl replied, "He wanted to know if the world was coming to an end."

In a sense I myself was one of the victims of the "Halloween prank" as Orson later called it in a masterly understatement. After listening to the broadcast in my apartment, I went to sleep blissfully unaware of what was happening outside. Later that night Houseman called to break the news, but I was too exhausted to hear the phone ring. The next morning I walked down 72nd Street from my apartment on Riverside Drive on my way to a barbershop. There was an air of excitement among the passersby. Catching ominous snatches of conversation with words like *invasion* and *panic,* I jumped to the conclusion that Hitler had invaded some new territory and that the war we all dreaded had finally broken out.

When I questioned the barber anxiously, he grinned. "Haven't you heard?" He held up the front page of a morning newspaper with the headline, "NATION IN PANIC FROM MARTIAN RADIO BROAD-CAST."

I stared at the paper while the confused barber stared at me. Center page was a picture of Orson, his arms outstretched in a gesture of helpless innocence, and underneath was the opening scene of my play. How the paper got hold of my script I have no idea; I heard later that the police had rushed into the studio at the end of the show and seized whatever copies they could find.

For twenty-four hours after the broadcast our fates hung in the balance. The public couldn't make up its collective mind whether we were heroes or villains. Finally Dorothy Thompson, in her influential column, ventured the opinion that we had done the country a service by showing how vulnerable we were to a panic reaction in the event of a real war. From then on the tide turned in our favor, and the course of all our lives was changed.

The Mercury Theatre, whose brilliant production of my play had brought about this explosive result, soon disbanded. Orson, an instant world celebrity, transported most of the Mercury players to Hollywood and made the classic *Citizen Kane* as producer, actor, and director. As for the screenplay on which it was based, Pauline Kael in *The New Yorker* revealed that John Houseman and Herman Mankiewicz had actually done much of the work for which Orson was credited. However, as in the case of *War of the Worlds* and the other Mercury plays, *Citizen Kane* was undoubtedly Orson's conception, both in subject matter and in method. I think it could be said of their close relationship over the years that Houseman was the pedestal on which the statue of Orson was erected. This is not to detract from Orson's theatrical flair. I would rank him as one of the great showmen of all time.

His resonant voice alone, with its telling inflections, is an incomparable dramatic instrument: an ordinary line of dialogue, such as his reply to the commentator's question about the gas eruptions on the planet Mars, "Mr. Philips, I cannot account for it," became immediately filled with portentous meaning.

Unfortunately, after their initial ventures in Hollywood, Orson and Houseman came to a parting of the ways and I feel this marked a decline in Orson's career, not as a public personality but as an artist. His later films became progressively more exhibitionist, with flashes of technical brilliance and originality but lacking the conviction to give a unifying point of view toward his subject matter; it seemed as though the magician in Orson had overtaken the serious filmmaker.

For me, the broadcast was a stroke of fortune. My arrangement with the Mercury group provided that I would forgo any immediate writing credit since the show was built around Orson's name in accordance with an agreement with CBS. However, as a further compensation for my small salary, I was accorded the residual ownership of the scripts that I wrote, none of us knowing at the time that one of them would become extremely valuable. We all kept our agreements, and the copyright of my *War of the Worlds* radio play is in my name with the various benefits that have since accrued.

Over the years the play has been collected in numerous journals and textbooks and reproduced in various media here and abroad. The Princeton social psychology department, under the direction of Hadley Cantril, did a comprehensive study of the panic, its causes and effects, the first of its kind on the subject. In book form, published by the Princeton University Press, it has gone into many editions. The record sale of the broadcast is approaching the million mark and a new edition is now being prepared to mark its fortieth anniversary.

The script has even been bootlegged. In Lima, Peru, a copy of the play was translated into Spanish and produced on a local radio station, spawning another panic; a number of its victims mobbed the radio station and burned it to the ground. More recently, in Buffalo, New York, the play was broadcast, unknown to us, causing mini-panic in that city.

Mars, it appears, is an uninhabited planet, but the fictional Martians we created changed my life, geographically as well as professionally. At the end of six months I left the Mercury program for a new venture, not without some regrets and misgivings. An easterner by birth and education, I had never been west of the Mississippi. My destination had a magic name: Hollywood.

PRECARIOUS PARADISE

It was a cold March day in 1939 when I locked the door of my Manhattan apartment on Riverside Drive. Outside, a chilly wind from the Hudson River was sucking the air from my lungs, and by the time I reached Grand Central I had left behind any regrets. At that time railroads still had some pride in their trains. The Twentieth Century Limited, overnight to Chicago, and the Santa Fe Chief, completing the trip to Los Angeles, were names to conjure with, like Europe's Orient Express. Down the long station platform leading to the sleek silver cars was a red carpet to save our tender eastern feet the shock of walking on cold cement: Magic Carpet.

Three days and sixty degrees Fahrenheit later the Santa Fe Chief snaked its way down through the Cajon Pass into the lush green and gold San Bernardino Valley. I'm always surprised when

the clichés that have been overused to describe a place turn out
to be true. My arrival in Los Angeles was a triumph of nature
over cynicism. There it was—just the way the posters pictured it.
With my useless topcoat slung over my shoulder, I walked from
the train into the open patio of Union Station, more Spanish than
Spain. The California sun was indecently warm on my winter
skin. The seductive fragrance of the yellow-blooming acacia trees
freighted the air, still untainted by smog. I stood staring at flowers that had no right to be out this early in the year—beds of
poppies, petunias, and African daisies, with blood-red bougainvillea festooning the ersatz adobe walls. Across the square from
the station was Olvera Street with its festive booths, tequila bars,
and guitar music, more Mexican than Mexico.

John Huston, an old friend, was there to meet me. It was a combination of his efforts and the Martian episode that brought me
to Hollywood to write for the Warner brothers. On the way to
my hotel we passed an orange grove. John stopped the car. "Pick
one." I did. Unlike the forbidden apple in the original Garden, a
stolen orange was the ritual entrance into Eden, California-style.

John had reserved a room for me at the Château Elysée in the
heart of Hollywood. The impressive building with its Norman
towers was a California adaptation of the châteaus in the Loire
Valley but was somewhat misplaced under a hill dominated by a
huge sign that spelled out HOLLYWOODLAND. John said he wanted
me to start my movie career there, as he had, because he felt it
had brought him luck. After having written several highly successful screenplays for Warners he was now on his way to becoming a director.

I later discovered that the Elysée was widely known in the
movie colony as the "Easy-Lay," which may or may not explain
the "luck" that John was wishing me.

That night I dined with the Hustons in their mountaintop
home overlooking a Hollywood valley so brilliantly lit with its
neon and strobe lights that the heavenly stars paled by compari-
son. A number of searchlights were crisscrossing the night sky

demanding our attention. A wide-eyed novitiate, I was willing to be impressed.

"Must be a big opening. What picture is it?"

"Probably a laundry or a delicatessen." John's wife, Leslie, had no intention of nurturing my illusions.

The home, typically California-modern, reflected his success. On three walls of the living room were paintings of the French Impressionists. The fourth wall was glass. On a clear day you could see Catalina. Jutting out over the sloping desert terrain was a grass terrace and the inevitable swimming pool. Like the homes of many of the movie colony elite hacked out of the Hollywood Hills, its hold on the sandy cliff seemed precarious. I still shudder to think what would happen if the San Andreas Fault, running underneath, ever decided to give these hills a hard jolt. Sunset Boulevard, down below, would be inundated by the wreckage of a thousand luxury homes.

Just a few days before my arrival John had lost his pet bullfrog, bitten by a rattlesnake in the desert brush only fifty yards from the house. That night when I was back at my hotel, I tried to sum up my first impressions of Hollywood: the juxtaposition of the highly civilized Huston home and a poisonous snake seemed to provide an appropriate symbol. A precarious paradise. Eden, yes, even to the serpent. That impression remained with me the next twelve years I spent there writing for films. But with all its faults, Hollywood was the undisputed movie capital of the world. By chance I was there at its height; I was also witness to the beginning of its decline and fall.

The next morning John drove me to the Warner studio in Burbank where I was assigned a corner office in the writers' building and a young woman from the secretarial pool anxious to be of service. Among her secretarial equipment was an electric stove.

"Make you some coffee?"

"No, thanks, I had breakfast." I pointed to a stack of yellow pads on my desk and a dozen Eagle pencils, my favorite to this day. They were all sharpened to a fine point, poised for action.

"When do I begin and on what?"

She laughed. "When you're new here, they don't rush you into an assignment unless you're a high-salaried writer."

My salary was three hundred a week—a fortune to me after my seventy-five hard-earned dollars at Mercury but a pittance by Hollywood standards.

"How do you know I'm not a high-salaried writer?"

"Oh, everybody knows everything here. Anyway, you'll want to look around the lot. It's pretty interesting."

I needed no urging; moviemaking had for me an element of magic. At that time, unlike today when movie tours are part of the business at Universal, visitors were not admitted to the "back lot" unless they were VIP guests of the studio heads. And here I was on the inside, free to roam where I pleased. I found myself on a "western street"—ramshackle buildings, stables, a jail, a sheriff's office, saloons, the familiar territory of outlaws and shoot-outs. Tombstone today, Virginia City tomorrow.

Turning a corner, I was in London. The street looked so real I had to peek behind the structures to be certain the "houses" were only fronts created by ingenious craftsmen, mostly out of Beaverboard and papier-mâché. I passed a pond with several miniature sailing vessels that could be transformed by camera trickery into full-sized ships at sea. On one side was a huge wind machine that could blow up a storm when needed.

Beyond the pond was an open area with bushes, a miniature forest, and a small swamp. At that time most outdoor shooting was done, not on location, but right there on the back lot. Though I didn't know it at the time, this swamp area was to be the "Panama jungle" where Errol Flynn and his band of English privateers would be ambushed by Spanish soldiers in my script of *The Sea Hawk*.

Most of the giant barnlike stages had a "NO VISITORS" warning; I hadn't yet learned that this sign could be disregarded if you acted as though you belonged on the set and stayed quiet during the shooting. Later I was to spend a great deal of time on these stages, and I never ceased to marvel at the amount of coordinated effort (and patience, as there was much waiting between setups) on the part of so many artists, technicians, and stagehands required to turn out three or four minutes of film in a working day. Each person had his special task and knew it well, from the star on camera to the gaffer operating the huge lamps on the scaffolding above the set.

Actors in all manner of dress peopled the narrow streets between the tall stages. I tried to guess which of the current productions fitted their costumes. Stars rode in motorized carts and one I identified from her pictures—Olivia de Havilland, even more beautiful than her image on the screen. And she smiled at me as she passed! It was like being recognized by a queen.

Back at the writers' building my secretary looked up from her desk in the outer office. "How did you like it?"

"Great, but . . . well, strange, a little scary."

She smiled. "You'll get used to it."

Would I? I wasn't so sure. I went into my office, facing those unused pencils and that empty pad. Did I really belong here in this make-believe world of artifice, of fronts with no third dimension, of life played out on sets that could be dismantled overnight and transformed into another place and another time? From my first view I wasn't even certain where the studio lot ended and the outside landscape began. I might arrive one morning and find they had taken down the mountain backdrop—which, however, proved to be the Hollywood Hills and relatively substantial, barring an earthquake.

And what of Olivia's smile? Was it her role, something that could be "taken down" at a word from a director and transformed into whatever expression the scene called for? When she left the studio at night, could she be certain of what she really felt as distinct from emotions she had learned to simulate? Did the two worlds, the imagined and the real, the public and the private, merge and become indistinguishable?

I had lived for over thirty years in one world; how would I fit into another? Playing my life backward through its various stages, I felt an urge to trace my present situation to its sources. While many things that happened to me along the way seemed accidental, was there a hidden design, a logical progression of events and experiences that brought me here? Perhaps the past would provide clues to whether or not I could adapt to this new environment and meet its demands. I had no story assigned to me by the studio, so I decided to use my own life as material and tell it as though I were writing it for the screen, a sort of practice session before the real work began.

John had given me one of his scripts to study screenplay form, and I had glanced through it and learned some of its terminology. I picked up one of the sharpened pencils and wrote down on my pad the first word—FLASHBACK.

BEGINNINGS

FADE IN

EXTERIOR: A STREET ON THE EDGE OF A SMALL UPSTATE NEW YORK CITY
separated from Hollywood by three thousand miles and a conservative life-style that goes back three centuries. With memory as a camera, we pick up a BOY of five huddled against his front door, gazing timidly at two neighbor boys across the road pumping a bicycle tire.

Born on a busy street of New York's East Side, I had assumed that the whole world was made of brick and cement and populated by older people. Now I found myself on an unpaved street of sparse frame houses and, beyond, wide open country, which up to then I had seen only in pictures. Bewildered and frightened, I was unwilling to venture out of doors without my parents.

All sorts of unknown perils might be lurking in the tall field grass and the dark, forbidding woods. And those two neighbor boys, slightly older than I, were staring at me from their lawn. They were dressed differently and had short hair. I had low bangs, Buster Brown–style. My mother said, "Go out and play with them." I had never played with another boy and hadn't the slightest idea how to go about it. I tried to slip back into the house but my mother had wisely locked the door. I doubt if it took Caesar more determination to cross the Rubicon than for me to cross that road. I still remember my opening gambit. "I came on a train and we crossed a bridge." The older boy said, "We know, we been to New York." The ice was broken. They took me on a tour of the neighborhood, showing me off—"the kid from New York with the funny haircut."

We had moved to Kingston where my father took an investigative job with the New York Board of Water Supply. This sleepy upstate city and its environs were once the hunting grounds of the Esopus Indians, but it was the settlers from Holland who left a lasting mark on the city with their charming houses of native fieldstone and their Old Dutch Church, whose graceful steeple still commands the landscape. Kingston's "society" was composed of their descendants. Unless your name had a "Van" in front of it, or the equivalent, you didn't belong. Although I played with their children, my parents were excluded from this tight, select circle on two scores: they were newcomers, and their ancestry was German-French instead of Dutch. Middle-class, I suppose, was our proper social category; we hung precariously to our bourgeois status by the grace of my father's white collar.

My mother was a handsome woman and my father a good-looking man. Outside of their possible physical attraction, I have no idea how they came to marry, as two people more unlike could hardly be imagined. My father was a born lawyer but without degree or portfolio. He may well have been the only person who ever read the twenty volumes of the *Encyclopaedia Britannica* from cover to cover. And his memory for what he read was prodigious. His mind was programmed with more facts than an IBM computer. Sometimes their sheer bulk would create a mental block inhibiting any effective action in a crisis. I remember an incident that was worthy of a Keystone comedy, although my father never appreciated the humor.

Rather late in his life he bought a car and was learning to drive it when I arrived from Hollywood for a visit. He seized upon me as a convenient driving instructor, although it was difficult to tell who was the teacher and who the student since he kept up a running account of what he had learned from the instructions that came with the car. It soon became evident that he knew all the rules of the road except how to stay on it.

After a few skirmishes, I began to dread those driving lessons. My father had certain unfortunate tendencies. One was to speed up at the street crossings on the theory that if he got through fast enough, we were unlikely to be hit by the cross traffic. The other danger spot was in turning a corner. In his anxiety to do it properly, he'd pull so hard on the wheel that we'd begin making a 180-degree turn. To avoid running up on the sidewalk, I'd grab the wheel and make the correction.

After one of these hazardous excursions, when nothing more serious had occurred than scraping a farmer's stone wall, we were back in Kingston heading down Washington Avenue, only a few blocks from home. It was a wide, straight street, and, feeling relatively safe, I relaxed against the seat and closed my eyes, thankful that the ordeal was nearly over. But I looked up to discover we had leaped the curb and were speeding across the well-manicured lawns of some of Kingston's more imposing residences. Ash cans went flying; saplings would appear briefly and then go down as though struck by a hurricane. Desperately, I pulled on the hand brake, but my father's foot was frozen on the gas pedal. We cut a swath through every lawn on the block before I could bring the rampaging machine to a stop in the middle of a large flower bed. The car was so bedecked with dahlias and geraniums that we could have entered the Pasadena Rose Parade.

By this time the good housewives up and down the block were rushing out to view the holocaust. For a half-minute my father just sat there, perhaps hoping it would all turn out to be a bad dream. There was nothing in his book of rules to tell him what to do in this situation. On my part, I was so convulsed with laughter I was of no use whatsoever. He gave me a disgusted look, climbed out of the car, picked his way through the uprooted flowers, and slowly approached the indignant housewives.

I turned to look out the car window, curious to hear how he would explain this unscheduled appearance on their front lawns. Only my father could have carried it off in this particular way. He picked up one of the ash cans, crushed flat, and holding it up toward the lady who owned it, remarked in his factual tone, "It couldn't have been in very good condition."

This was too much even for the housewives. How can you be angry with a man capable of passing off a near catastrophe by implying that a more durable ash can might have withstood the assault? Unable to contain my laughter, I rolled out of the car, and by this time the ladies were laughing too. Only my father remained unmoved. He stood there, broken ash can in hand, wondering what was so funny.

At the opposite extreme, my mother was Madame Bovary, American provincial instead of French. She lived in the world of the might-have-been and the might-still-be. Excluded from the small-town "aristocracy" of Kingston, in her imagination she hurdled over it into the high society of the Four Hundred. From Cholly Knickerbocker's gossip column she kept track of their doings and misdoings, of debutantes' coming-out parties, their marriages, and the scandals that usually followed these alliances of wealth. She lived vicariously in the baronial mansions of the Astors, the Belmonts, and Vanderbilts in Newport, Tuxedo Park, and Southampton that were infinitely more important to her than the prosaic everyday life of a small-town housewife.

Like many romantic women of the period (but unlike Madame Bovary), my mother, I'm quite certain, remained technically faithful. Her occasional flirtations were carefully circumscribed by late-Victorian conventions. One summer—I was twelve or thirteen—we took frequent excursions on the *Elihu Bunker,* a small Hudson River boat that plied between Poughkeepsie and Kingston. Its cargo was mostly fruit picked up at the various farming towns on the way, but it also accommodated a few passengers, and often my mother and I were the only ones making the round trip.

The pilot and owner, Captain Blodgett, was an attractive man, lean and tanned, with the intense blue eyes that seem to go with sea- and river-faring men. Although my knowledge of sex was incredibly scant for my age, I sensed that something was going on between my mother and the captain that she wished to keep secret. I was being used as a sort of chaperone, although I couldn't then define my role.

However, I was given one duty on the boat which I did understand and which made the trips worthwhile. Captain Blodgett taught me how to steer the ship, and after a while he allowed me regular turns at the wheel where the river required no special knowledge of navigation. He would instruct me, "Hold her on that lighthouse until you're within a hundred yards or so, then change your course and make for that point up yonder." When he was sure I understood, he would leave and go out on the stern deck with my mother.

Alone in the pilothouse with the safety of the ship resting on my young shoulders, I felt a wonderful sense of power and importance. It was a challenge to keep the *Bunker* straight on course, then swing the huge wheel as I picked up the next navigation point. After one of these exciting trips, I wanted to impress my father with my accomplishment, but I sensed that my mother preferred me not to bring up the subject.

If I'm a sort of hybrid, half realist, half romantic, I come by it honestly, wedged in between the conflicting attitudes and desires of my parents. My father naturally assumed I would be a lawyer, fulfilling the ambition he had not quite achieved.

My mother had other plans for me. She wasn't so concerned with what profession I followed so long as I "amounted to something." Actually, she was aiming me toward a glamorous life that had been denied her. The zigzagging of my early career was probably the result of a subconscious desire to please both my parents. In their own way they did their best for me, each making me feel I had some mission to fulfill in the years ahead, but with different concepts as to the nature of that mission.

Despite its stuffiness and backwardness (the population had hardly changed since the Civil War), Kingston was an ideal American community for a boy's growing-up years. In one direction from our home on the western fringe of town, a fifteen-minute walk east on Main Street took me to "downtown," with many attractions: the Greek candy kitchen (ice cream cones a nickel, licorice a penny a string), the Bijou Movie House (admission a dime), special occasions like Circus Day in the spring when school was let out at eleven o'clock so that we could watch the parade. My friends and I perched like sparrows on the iron fence around the Old Dutch Church graveyard. On those moldering tombstones was written part of our history—the names and dates of early Dutch settlers alongside the British and American soldiers of the Revolutionary War, sharing the ground they had once fought over. One of the stones bearing the name of my closest friend was so eroded by time and weather we could hardly read the carved inscription: "Here lyes Severyn Bruyn, born 1650, died 1706. Rest in peace." My friend Severyn Bruyn, alias "Pete," used to leapfrog over his great-great-grandfather's gravestone to demonstrate what a lively corpse he was.

Once I had overcome my initial city-bred fears, the great adventure of my boyhood lay in the opposite direction. Westward from our house was open country unending—it might have stretched to the Pacific Ocean for all I knew. A few nearby farms and beyond them no habitations, just fields and woods and streams that seemed to belong to no one and therefore were ours by right of discovery and possession. Even the names I remember were evocative and inviting: "Joy's Woods," "Frog Pond," "Green Hill," "Ringtop," and "The Beaverkill" celebrated in the writings of the naturalist John Burroughs.

The seasons ran in our blood, each month beguiling us with a new attraction. Windy March was obviously made for flying kites; in April came the first balmy morning when we were allowed to go coatless to school, a baseball glove strapped to our books and hidden in our desks until the recess bell rang. By May violets were purpling the fields and we picked them for our parents if they were in good standing, or we took them up to Wall Street and sold them to passersby for ten cents a bunch. The summer months were for exploring the woods, fishing, and dreaming, the autumn for gathering hickory and butternuts and for stealing pumpkins from the stacked cornfields. In November, Frog Pond froze for skating, and soon the leafless landscape turned white with the aging year. Converting barrel staves into skis, we plunged down the steep slope of Ringtop, occasionally reaching the bottom upright, but more often landing headfirst in a snowbank since none of us knew the art of traversing to break our speed.

Having no brothers or sisters, I gravitated toward large families: the Bruyns with three children, the Burgevins with nine—a ready-made baseball team. I became a sort of surrogate brother, spending more time in their homes than in my own. I learned to play their games and gradually picked up their lore of the woods and fields. My mother's complaint changed: "You're never home anymore."

There were girls, of course, and they intrigued me, but I was wary of them. They seemed to know so much more. Obviously they were different from boys, but I couldn't figure out just what made the difference. The word *sex* was not in common currency those days, so one had to puzzle this out with no help from parents or teachers.

One rainy day I was playing with a friend in the upstairs room of her home. Tiring of playing boys' games, she stretched out on the floor and looked at me, smiling. I sensed an invitation and lay down beside her, unbuttoning her blouse and exploring her body, having no idea what I was looking for. Her little nipples were no different from mine. Farther down in the middle of her stomach was a belly button, but I had one too. This was as far as I got. I was about to pull down her bloomers when Mrs. G., probably made suspicious by the silence, opened the door, her face flushed with anger. Ruth was ordered to get back into her clothes, and I was sent home in disgrace, the mystery still unsolved.

That little experiment made me shy of girls and retarded my sex life more years than I care to admit. I didn't even fall in love until I was nine years old. It happened during a game of post office. Polly Bruyn, Pete's sister, a girl my age, was waiting behind a curtain when I drew the forfeit, which meant I had to kiss her. It was another Rubicon. I think I would have been less timid had there been a lion on the other side of the curtain instead of a pretty girl. But there was no backing down without being in disgrace with all the kids in the neighborhood, so I screwed up my courage, went behind the curtain, and pecked her on the cheek. The effect was astonishing. I had the sensation of tasting some delicious sweetness like the nectar I imagined the hummingbird sipped inside the petals of our trumpet vine. In my euphoria I decided Polly was my girl and staked my claim by giving her a pencil (no Freudian implications in those more innocent days). Unfortunately, Polly was not as committed as I was, and before long I caught her flirting with one of my rivals. I marched up to her room and demanded my pencil back. And so ended my first love affair.

CUT FLASHBACK

TIME: THE PRESENT

My office window at Warners opened on palm and acacia trees
where a mockingbird had chosen to nest. If you have a mockingbird, you don't need any other—he knows the whole repertoire of
bird songs and this one could even imitate a GI's flirtatious whis-
tle to attract a passing girl.

Those first weeks at the studio it seemed as though I had been
admitted to an earthly paradise, even though the keeper of the
front gate who marked our comings and goings was a cop and
not a guardian angel. I had free time to do as I pleased. The
other writers I met were friendly and went out of their way to
make me feel I belonged, even though I was still without an
assignment. I had visited all the stages and explored every corner
of the lot and was becoming a little restless. I talked over my
situation with a fellow writer, Dalton Trumbo, later to become a
leader of the now-famed Hollywood Ten. Dalton was a man without illusions.

"The front office likes to type writers, actors, everybody. It
saves them from having to do any original thinking, which isn't
their strong point. In your case they've probably typed you as a
Martian and they're not making pictures about Martians."

"What can I do?"

Dalton gave it some thought. "You've done other things beside
those radio shows. Dig something out of your experiences and
try to interest them. Make it simple so they can understand it."

Back in my office, I decided to follow Dalton's advice. Out of
my various doings and misdoings, there must be something that
would provide material for the screen. I had practiced law, or
perhaps mispracticed it would be more accurate, with some resulting situations that were comic, at least from my current per-

spective. And as a college student I had even preached one summer in a country church. Back to my phantom script.

FADE IN

INT. CLASSROOM
in a small college located in Annandale-on-the-Hudson. Camera (memory) favors a young STUDENT dressed in an academic gown translating, Greek to English, passages from Xenophon's *Anabasis*, recounting the bold sortie of a small Greek army into the heart of the Persian Empire. Seated at his desk, nodding his head, is a gentle, soft-spoken PROFESSOR, his face the color and texture of old parchment, looking as ancient as the language he is teaching.

At the tender age of sixteen I entered St. Stephen's (later renamed Bard College) as the youngest freshman, and probably the most immature, in its eighty-year history. Carved out of the old patroon estates, St. Stephen's was richly endowed by nature and by now Bard has become one of the most educationally advanced of our small colleges. During my stay nearly all of its hundred or so students were postulants for the Episcopalian ministry. Evening chapel service was compulsory unless you could bribe the attendance marker, which I frequently did—not with money but by writing his English compositions.

The curriculum was molded along the classical lines of Oxford, requiring four years of Latin and Greek. Since I had a somewhat dubious talent for analyzing what my professors wanted and giving it back to them on tests, it took me only a semester to establish myself as an outstanding student. My daily routine was classroom to tennis court, the only places I could excel and compensate for my social and emotional inadequacies.

Since most of my fellow students were preparing for a career in the church, much of the common room discussions centered on abstruse ecclesiastical subjects like the Trinity, which I never understood, and the Immaculate Conception, even more mysterious as I wasn't even familiar with the requirements of normal conception. As the lone prelaw student, I was pretty much the odd man out.

Being the college "baby" added to my problems, especially where girls were concerned. On the rare dance weekends when girls were allowed on campus, I would usually manage to bring a pretty girl since, my home being just across the river, I had a wider choice. However, she would immediately be monopolized by the stags waiting like jackals on the sidelines. Less adept at the art of flirtation, I was an easy mark for these predators. While I would be suffering through my duty dances with the faculty wives, my date would be off kicking her heels with the football crowd.

One of the illusions I brought with me to college was the belief that one had to be "called" to the ministry in a literal sense, by hearing the voice of God. Some of the more devout of my fellow students confirmed this belief and were dedicated to a spiritual life, but I discovered that the vast majority were going into the church for the same worldly reasons one might enter any profession. I remember how shocked I was when I first heard them talk about the social prestige enjoyed by a minister and the opportunities his position in the community afforded him to "make a good marriage," meaning a wealthy one. And politics played a part—one had to "stand in well" with the right bishop to obtain a lucrative rectorship of an important church.

Among this group, Arthur P., a junior during my freshman year, was an outstanding practitioner. Short and stocky, dark-visaged, a persuasive talker who buttonholed his listeners, Arthur was typecast for a ward heeler, even to the cigar permanently embedded in a corner of his mouth. If he had gone into politics, he would surely have wheeled and dealed his way into Congress. On Sundays he was the lay reader (a sort of semiminister) of a small rural church in the nearby hamlet of Barrytown, a sinecure he had somehow inveigled out of the New York diocese although his home was in Rhode Island. Anxious to keep his job and the fifteen dollars it brought him each Sunday, he had to find a substitute to hold it for him during the summer months while he was away on vacation. Since I lived just across the river and was not likely to appropriate his "cathedral," he settled on me.

I objected strenuously. I had no idea how to conduct a service and I was scared to death of appearing before an audience. But Arthur, as I said, was persuasive—and an upperclassman, which gave him considerable leverage over a lowly freshman. Besides, the weekly fee of fifteen dollars, a substantial sum in those days, would allow me to spend six days a week in an idle, tennis-playing summer.

Under his instruction I learned the order of service, when and what to pray, when hymns were to be sung and the sermon preached. He loaned me his book of sermons, mostly dry, innocuous elaborations of a biblical text. By church law a lay reader was required to preach only a "canned" sermon.

After the commencement exercises in June, the dreaded Sunday came for my first appearance at the rustic church; I fervently wished that I could contract typhoid fever or something equally debilitating. But I was in the prime of health and had no excuse. In the closet-sized sacristy I put on my black cassock, covering my trembling knees. Preceded by a small, disdainful acolyte carrying a silver cross—a ten-year-old who obviously knew much more than I about the ritual—I made my entrance to the altar. The congregation, thirty or forty souls, all rose to their feet, taking me by surprise so that I couldn't think how to get them seated again and the service off the ground. I fumbled for the opening words in the prayer book and delivered what was probably the most inaudible invocation ever uttered in an Episcopal church.

I don't know how much spiritual guidance my congregation received that first Sunday, but at least they got plenty of exercise. I hardly had them on their knees when, in my nervousness,

I prematurely signaled the organist, who blasted out the first chord of the opening hymn. The surprised parishioners bobbed to their feet, then down again as I corrected the mistake and resumed the prayers. When the time for the sermon came, I didn't think I had the strength to climb to the pulpit. Somehow I managed to get there, where I gave the congregation a very unconvincing blessing and plunged into the canned sermon. As my confidence increased, my voice grew stronger and I got through the rest of the service without mishap.

After the service it is customary for the preacher to shake hands with the parishioners as they file out of church. Dutifully, each of them told me how much he had enjoyed the sermon, which wasn't much of a compliment since it wasn't mine. However, they were kind and friendly, no doubt making allowances for my extreme youth and perhaps somewhat relieved that I didn't reek of stale cigars like my predecessor, known on campus as the "bishop."

Most of my "flock" were country people of slender means, the majority of them violet growers, the prevailing horticulture of this section of Dutchess County. But it seems in every Episcopal parish there is at least one wealthy family whose contributions are its main support. Often they occupy a special pew with their name on a brass plate. In this instance the family was the Zabriskies, whose huge ancestral estate with its manor house overlooking the Hudson (now a part of the Bard campus) had come down to them from an original settler under the semifeudal patroon system. Together with their neighboring estate owners— the Astors, the Delanos, the Roosevelts, and the Livingstons— they kept alive an aristocratic tradition longer than most other segments of American society. In the case of the Livingstons, the original grant included "all the land west to the Pacific Ocean" with a blithe disregard for the native inhabitants. When it was discovered that the ocean was some three thousand miles away, the Livingstons found it impractical to enforce the entire grant, but they did pretty well, their domain at one time extending to Livingston Manor in Orange County.

This is perhaps enough background to appreciate my second ordeal of the day. The Zabriskies, out of pity or custom or curiosity that such a callow youth would venture to preach to them, invited me to dinner at the manor house. All I wanted was to go home and relax, but to refuse would have been a breach of my pastoral duties.

The Zabriskies were a storybook family. The elderly widowed mother looked and behaved like a somewhat eccentric dowager empress. Her daughter, son-in-law, and their children were all handsome with the easy, natural manners of those so accustomed to the advantages of wealth that they feel no need to impress. Their guests were the sort of sophisticated people one would expect to find in such a household—with the single exception of myself.

Before dinner, sherry was served by a butler on the veranda overlooking the formal gardens that terraced down to the river. I felt as though I was on a stage set playing a role for which I hadn't learned the lines. If I added a dozen words to the general conversation, I'm sure they were not notable for their urbanity or wit. As the visiting "pastor" I felt I was expected to strike a note of spiritual or moral uplift, but for the life of me, I couldn't think what. Most of the talk centered on castles and châteaus they had visited in various parts of the world. Since my range of traveling was roughly a hundred miles, I had nothing to offer but an attentive ear.

The dinner, as I remember it, was a prolonged agony from the terrapin bisque to the meringue glacé. Seated next to the formidable Mrs. Zabriskie, who absentmindedly kept dropping her napkin on the floor, I spent at least a third of the meal under the table retrieving it. Sometimes I would stay down there among the well-shod legs longer than necessary for a few breaths of unsophisticated air, only coming up when I felt my absence would be noticed. The dinner conversation darted around the table like a hummingbird, too fast for me to intercept with the brilliant witticisms I was desperately struggling to improvise. When the ordeal was over and I was dispatched to the ferry in their limousine, I thought of the clever things I might have said, but I couldn't very well send them back with the chauffeur.

At the other end of the economic scale among my parishioners was an elderly spinster, Mary Jane Ricks. The phrase "poor as a church mouse" was applicable, since she spent most of her time in the little church and she was spectacularly poor. Her poverty was on public display in the two pennies she dropped noisily into the collection plate and it shrieked at you when you visited her ramshackle yellow house up the road from the church. A half-dozen venerable hens pecked away around the broken-down doorstep. Even the altar flowers she brought from her garden were faded and scrawny. But Mary Jane, wearing a long black Sunday dress and an old-fashioned bonnet, was the soul of kindness and I'm certain a more Episcopalian woman never lived.

Except in church, where she was properly solemn, she chuckled at almost everything I said, which helped to restore my damaged ego. She took an instant liking to me—or perhaps she would have idolized anyone who occupied the pulpit, however precariously. But the price I had to pay for this idolatry was to dine at her house every other Sunday, she and the Zabriskies taking turns. I don't know which I dreaded more—the opulent feast at the manor house or the tough, stringy chicken with heavily larded gravy at Mary Ricks's. Out of the goodness of her heart she would slaughter those ancient hens, one by one, in my honor, although they were almost her only possessions. Each visit I used to look at the survivors and wonder whether they and I would last out the summer. When I protested to my hostess not to kill any more for my sake but to preserve them for their eggs, she chuckled and said they'd stopped laying years ago.

Miss Ricks was probably as old as her chickens and slightly dotty because she told me she saw angels hovering over my head when I preached the canned sermons. In fact she was so insistent that I got to giving quick glances over my shoulder just on the chance. I never found an angel there, but I discovered something about myself: I enjoyed preaching! Perhaps it would be more accurate to say I enjoyed the effect I could create on my audience. Like an actor learning his trade, I began to experiment with meaningful pauses and gestures and developed certain tricks with my voice to dramatize the points I was making.

Finding that the dry, warmed-over sermons didn't provide much opportunity for histrionics, I began to make changes in the texts, at first just a word or two, then sentences and paragraphs. I remember having a moment's pause when one Saturday I found myself rewriting the Easter sermon of the dean of the Cathedral of St. John the Divine. But I was basking in the warm response of my congregation. The Zabriskies were even bringing their week-end guests to hear the "boy preacher" and dear old Mary Ricks was seeing more angels than ever floating over my head. By the end of the summer I had discarded the book altogether and was writing my own sermons. I hope that the then head of the New York Episcopal Diocese, Bishop Manning, in the spirit of Christian charity will forgive my youthful presumption. At any rate it gave me intense satisfaction when the fall college term commenced and I returned the "cathedral" to "Bishop P." that I had increased his congregation by at least ten souls who might otherwise have perished in Episcopalian outer darkness.

In later years I came to realize that this ability to sway or influence people by the spoken word was a two-edged sword. It was an asset in the movie world and in political causes, but there were occasions when I have used it to get my way regardless of its consequences to others. This is not a propensity I recall with pride, but there it is—or was.

It was in my sophomore year at St. Stephen's that my real education began, one that went far beyond the mere acquisition of high marks. Taking my first sociology course, I had for my mentor a remarkable man, Dr. Lyford Edwards, a radical Episcopalian priest who had taken his doctorate in social science at the University of Wisconsin under Dr. Ross, then the acknowledged leader in his field. Dr. Edwards had come only recently to St. Stephen's, having spent the intervening years in what was rumored to be an adventurous life. His teaching method was to shock his students out of their complacency. He showed us how many of our assumptions about the society we lived in, whose virtue we had taken for granted, were false.

Soon I began to realize that nearly everything of any importance I had learned in the previous sixteen years had to be unlearned. Piece by piece, my neat little bourgeois world came apart. By the end of the semester, I stood among the wreckage wondering how I could rebuild with more durable materials.

During my next three years at St. Stephen's I took every course Dr. Edwards offered and became a sort of protégé. I was like a parched desert plant that had never tasted rain suddenly overtaken by a cloudburst. Beside giving his lectures and providing an enormous reading list which covered every sociological subject from the mores of the Australian aborigines to the extralegal manipulations of the international cartels, he sent his advanced students out into the field to discover for themselves what was behind the carefully groomed facade of our twentieth-century American civilization. We went into prisons, slum tenements, hospitals, morgues, old people's homes, insane asylums, immigrant compounds, and places of last resort such as the Bowery, searching out the roots of our social ills and the possible remedies.

In my rebellion against the lies and hypocrisies that had been fed to me, I went to the other extreme, seeking out the most uncomfortable truths and wearing them like a hair shirt. The more I observed the way most people lived and died, the more clear it seemed that, if God was in His heaven, He wasn't giving much thought to his earthly sparrows. I recalled the story of the youthful Gautama Buddha living in a high-walled, princely garden, protected from the knowledge of the evils that afflicted the outside world. In his eighteenth year, evading his teachers, he scaled the wall. Before he had wandered far from his palace—so the legend goes—he encountered poverty, disease, and death. The young prince never returned to his garden. For the rest of his life he practiced the philosophy of abnegation that bears his name. My reaction to the social evils I had encountered was neither princely nor resigned. Like my mentor I became a "radical," although as yet without a cause and with no definite goal.

I cheated my professor only once on those field trips. In my junior year Dr. Edwards proposed a research into the causes of prostitution. The information was to be gathered from working prostitutes. He didn't specify how we were to get the girls to disclose the circumstances leading to their fall from grace. This was up to us. He did admonish us on certain precautions in case we got carried away in our zeal for knowledge.

This posed a perplexing problem for me. I was proud of my standing with Dr. Edwards and I didn't want to fail in such an adventurous assignment. At the same time, I had practically no experience in sexual matters and I wasn't even sure I could recognize a prostitute if I met her on the street. Could I count on her wearing a scarlet dress? Or would she wiggle her hips suggestively and murmur, "Want to come with me, mister?" If she did, would I have the nerve to go? And if so, how would I broach the subject of her past when that was probably the last thing she'd want to talk about—if she wanted to talk at all?

Unable to resolve these questions, I decided to play it by ear and trust to luck. The first thing was to find a bona fide subject. I selected Greenwich Village as the most promising territory for the search. At nine in the evening I started walking the streets south from 14th. At two in the morning I was still walking. I may have passed a dozen prostitutes in those five hours but I had no way of being certain and a mistake could be serious. No girl accosted me, even though I did my best to look receptive. They may have thought I was too young to have ten dollars in my pocket, or whatever was the prevailing fee. At two o'clock I admitted defeat and went to bed alone, none the wiser in the ways of prostitutes.

On the train back to college the next morning, my older classmates were full of their night's exploits which were more sexual than sociological. If their stories were true, which I doubted, the confessional booths in our college chapel were going to be in demand the next few evenings. On my part, I maintained a cryptic silence—they could believe what they wished. Back at college, ashamed to admit my failure, I fabricated a long and revealing dialogue with an imaginary streetwalker. She was probably the most romantic prostitute in literature. Aside from her physical charms and her youth—she was barely sixteen and I was her first client—she was high-minded and very moral. She must have read Karl Marx because she had a clear understanding that her downfall was the result of the capitalist system. The mill in her hometown had shut down to break a strike, her father was unemployed, and her mother wasting away from tuberculosis. What could the girl do but come to the big city and sell the only possession she had left, her body? By the time I'd finished the paper, I was nearly in tears over her tragic plight. When later I confessed my fabrication to Dr. Edwards, he didn't seem surprised. He grinned and said my report was probably as accurate as any of the sob stories the girls would've handed me had I managed to run them down.

Today college radicals are something we take for granted, but there weren't many of us in the twenties, when the stock market was booming and the Horatio Alger American Dream was still intact. Our brand was less sophisticated and, although we did little about it, we talked social injustice to anyone who would listen—and no doubt succeeded in boring more than we converted. It was particularly hard on our families. On my visits home I gave my parents long and fervent lectures on what I'd just learned, expecting them to renounce the conventional beliefs they had lived with for forty years. My mother wasn't interested in my social ideas. High society, yes, but not this talk of slums and the other sins of capitalism. She just hoped it wouldn't get me into trouble. My father was plain angry. Who was I to tell him that the Democratic party wasn't the answer to all social problems and the friend of the common man? But all wasn't lost. My futile efforts to convert my family to radicalism became the subject of my first Broadway play.

Back to the present. Six weeks had passed at Warners and still no assignment, the front office apparently having forgotten the existence of their "Martian expert." After a while, unless you are doing something, even paradise can begin to pall. Also, I was aware that my option came due at the end of the next month. Credits are the lifeblood of screenwriters, and how could I earn a credit unless Somebody Up There gave me an assignment?

In my reminiscences I was learning a great deal about myself, even some uncomfortable truths, but I couldn't imagine the studio wanting to make a picture on the tribulations of an adolescent. Anyway, MGM had garnered that market with their Andy Hardy series. However, I had brought with me a copy of my first play, a family comedy that might possibly interest them. It had achieved a Broadway production through a series of convoluted circumstances, seemingly accidental. (Are we all the product of accident or am I particularly blessed—or cursed?) Probably the most unlikely road to the stage is through the law, but that is how it came about.

FADE IN

INT. A LAW OFFICE

on one of the four corners in the business section of Hartsdale in Westchester County where a recent GRADUATE of Columbia Law School had the presumption to start a private practice instead of joining an established law firm.

My first trial, which took place in the City Court of White Plains, was as much a debacle as my first service in the Barrytown church. The case was a simple matter of a debt owed my client by contract. I started to give a straightforward presentation of the facts in ordinary layman's terms. I soon discovered I was violating one of the sacred precepts of jurisprudence. The opposing lawyer was constantly on his feet catching me up in procedural errors and the judge was sustaining his objections. I floundered around for a while, getting into evidence about half of what I had intended, and then sat down in utter dejection, afraid to look at my client, whose feelings I could imagine.

The opposing lawyer now took over. Without any real substance to his defense, he made the most of his superior knowledge of the legalities. He began by pointing out that even my preliminary papers—the complaint and notice of trial—were incorrectly drawn. The judge agreed with him but mercifully gave me the right to amend them. Then the defense attorney put his client on the stand and, cleverly guiding his answers with leading questions, drew from him a distorted picture of the events leading to the contract. My client, by now furious, nudged me to do something. I did the only thing I could think of—I began to object to every question put by the opposing lawyer. Unfortunately, I hadn't any idea on what to base my objections. Taking pity on me, the judge sustained a few of my objections, supplying his own reasons. When the trial ended, the defendant and his attorney looked very pleased, while my client was so angry he wouldn't speak to me. That evening I went back to the office so dejected I was ready to tear down my "Attorney-at-Law" sign, which hung over the door.

An odd postscript to the debacle came a week later when the judge's decision arrived by mail, awarding judgment for the full amount to my client. Our case was so foolproof that all my blunders couldn't lose it. My client forgave me, but it took me a long time to forgive myself.

The other matter entrusted to me that first year was more serious, involving lives as well as money. Across the street from the
office stood an old frame house owned jointly by a middle-aged
woman and a younger man, a gardener; I shall call them Mrs.
West and Jack Kelsey. Mrs. West had originally purchased the
property for a small sum, but the town was now growing and
since the lot was situated on a prominent business corner, its
market value was around forty thousand dollars.

Mrs. West and Jack were living in so-called sin. When the
affair started, her infatuation with the younger man had impaired
her judgment, or perhaps he had imposed a condition before
entering the alliance. At any rate, she made the mistake of deed-
ing her lover a half interest in her home, which had unexpectedly
turned into a gold mine. The course of true love had become
anything but smooth. Their quarrels were violent. I often heard
them shouting at each other from my office across the street. An
affair so colorful and with such explosive possibilities was bound
to attract attention; the whole town was following its ups and
downs as though it were a World Series game.

One fateful day they appeared together at my office. They had
put on their best clothes and their best manners, evidently having
agreed to declare a truce in their private war long enough to present their problem to me with a show of dignity. Each wanted to
get free of the other, but the property they jointly owned bound
them together. If I needed any further proof of their incompati-
bility, it came during that first interview. After a tense but peace-
ful start the truce was forgotten, and each began cataloguing for
my benefit all the sins committed by the other—and the list was
long and impressive. After they had exhausted their recrimina-
tions and Mrs. West had shed some tears, I managed to calm
them down with the assurance that their difficulties would soon
be resolved.

How I was going to resolve them I had no idea. I went to the
Columbia law library to look up the laws on real property settle-

ments; to my dismay, I found them hedged by more technicalities than most other branches of law. What convolutions Blackstone hadn't thought of, various legislatures had since added in a bewildering array of statutes affecting the partitioning of property. The law was somewhat clearer on the rights of husband and wife, but my clients weren't married. To make matters more complicated, I wasn't even certain that the deed from Mrs. West to her lover was an effective instrument. Had there been a valid consideration? True, Jack had given several years of his youth, but I suspected this wasn't as valuable in the eyes of the law as the peppercorn so often referred to as consideration in early common law. As if that were not enough, it occurred to me that if the matter came to litigation, I would find myself representing both parties, which, to say the least, was questionable legal ethics.

I decided on the only course I could think of. Instead of dealing with my clients as a lawyer, I would become their marriage counselor, patch up their quarrels, and make them love each other again. Little did I realize what I was letting myself in for. Each took to coming in separately to confide in me the latest outrage of the other and to prod me into hastening their separation. Counseling patience and tolerance, I invented all sorts of virtues in the other partner that perhaps were being overlooked. Why not try to recapture the harmony and affection they must once have felt when they entered their relationship? Jack listened to me politely but with some skepticism. Mrs. West was more difficult. I suppose there is nothing more venomous than a love that has curdled. All she wanted was to get that so-and-so out of her house and to see him take as few of her earthly possessions as possible. When I tried to point out his virtues—his youth, his good looks, and his industry—she countered with a list of his infidelities that would make Casanova pale. It was clear that Jack was spending as much time in the bedrooms of his female customers as in their gardens. As time passed with no resolution to their problem and no real reconciliation, Mrs. West began bringing me bottles of homemade wine she had illicitly brewed, perhaps hoping it would stimulate me to action.

Finally a day came when the problem could no longer be put off. Early in the morning Jack burst into my office, trembling with rage and threatening to kill Mrs. West if he had to live with her another week. Nor was he going to leave the property without getting his share. God knows he'd earned it—and on and on. I didn't even try to conciliate. Half an hour later Mrs. West stormed in, equally furious, with her side of the story. If Jack didn't get out of her house before the week was up, she'd see him carried out feetfirst.

I was desperate. I envisioned poison being slipped into Jack's coffee if he didn't first plunge his pruning shears into his mistress's body. In either case I would have contributed to murder, and I didn't want that on my conscience. Suddenly an idea occurred to me. Instead of giving up the case in defeat, I would engage a consultant, as a general doctor might call in a specialist if the patient's condition became serious. A lawyer from nearby Scarsdale agreed to handle the matter for me. To my clients I built him up as an expert in real estate partitioning, although actually he was in general practice as I was. The only difference was that he knew his business. My clients had no objection—they would have agreed to anything to get the affair settled and see the last of each other. My consultant knew exactly what steps to take and the whole thing was over in a matter of a few days. I had saved face in the community but not with myself. My personal approach to law was more likely to become a public menace than a benefaction. I had to either learn the rules or give up the game. I decided that the game wasn't worth it.

Instead I started commuting to New York several evenings a week to see plays. The theatre had always intrigued me but now it began to overshadow everything else. It was the theatre of Eugene O'Neill, Sidney Howard, George Kaufman, Clifford Odets, and Robert Sherwood. And the men who produced their plays put their hearts as well as their money into them—unlike today's impersonal "packaging," financed by syndicates or millionaires creating tax losses.

On one of these trips I brought back a copy of George Kaufman's *Butter and Egg Man,* a slight, conventional comedy but constructed by an expert craftsman. I began to spend most of my working hours in the back room of the office taking the play apart, scene by scene, like an apprentice jeweler learning the mechanism of a watch. A friend, Emerson Evans, an inspired teacher and a frustrated playwright, was immersed in the literature of the theatre, but somehow his vast theoretical knowledge seemed to act as a block to his own writing. He would write a scene one day and tear it up the next, the critic canceling out the writer. I was fortunate in having Emerson as my literary mentor, filling in some of the large gaps in my lopsided education. It was like a crash course in drama for which I'm afraid I never amply repaid him before his untimely death.

Since I had none of Emerson's critical inhibitions, I became eager to apply what I had learned. His advice was to select material from my own experience: I seized on the idea of a young college student imposing his newly acquired radicalism on his hapless parents. It was intended as merely a practice effort, but Emerson insisted on taking my finished script to a producer. To my amazement he accepted it for production, first in a Springfield, Massachusetts, stock company and later on Broadway.

Two moments stand out in my memory of the Springfield opening—seeing my name as the author of the play on the bill outside the theatre and hearing the audience laugh for the first time at one of my lines. There can be only one "first." Nothing since then has quite equaled the thrill of that stock company production of my inconsequential play. Later it was produced on Broadway, where it received mixed notices and had a short run—which is all it deserved.

In some desperation I sent a copy of this play to the head of the Warners story department. A few days later I received this answer on an interoffice memo:

Thank you for sending me your play, "He Went to College." I'm afraid this is not the kind of story Warners wishes to produce at this time.

Walter MacEwen

Anyway, he was now aware of my existence and some time later he called me on the phone. Would I get in touch with Robert Buckner, a writer in our building, who was having trouble "licking a story" (an unfortunate Hollywood phrase that often reflected the literal truth) for a picture they wanted to do. I may be able to help him. I said yes, if Buckner was willing.

When I met him in his office, Bob Buckner was more than willing. An experienced screenwriter and later a producer, he had been struggling with material that just didn't seem to work into a dramatic form. We talked for several days and eventually it began to take some sort of shape. It was a run-of-the-mill western that had no interest for me except as an exercise in craftsmanship. My contribution was small, but Bob was pleased and generously offered me a second credit with the warm acquiescence of Mr. MacEwen.

I thanked them but refused. In many of my former activities— as preacher, teacher, lawyer—I had operated more by wits than by merit, doing jobs I was unprepared for, getting marks and money I hadn't really earned. And my reminiscing had reminded me of the times I had "grassed," scrounging off my family or friends. But upon becoming a writer, this had changed. It was to be my life's work, one area in which I had so far functioned with scrupulous honesty, and I wanted to keep it that way. I knew very well I hadn't earned that credit—it was offered me as a boost to my screen career. The credit I wanted was one I could rightly claim as my own.

THE SEA HAWK

It finally happened. On John Huston's recommendation, Henry
Blanke, Warners' most esteemed producer, sent me a thirty-page
treatment entitled *The Sea Hawk* with an interoffice memo: "This
is planned for Errol Flynn's next picture. Please read it and, if
interested in doing the screenplay, contact me."

What a windfall! A top producer and Warners' biggest box-
office star, not the usual project entrusted to an untried, low-
salaried writer. It must have required much persuasion on John's
part for Blanke to take the chance.

The treatment was typical Flynn fare, physical action galore
but not much in the way of characterization, nuances, or credibility even on its own romantic terms. I was in a dilemma. I
needed the credit badly, but was this the kind of credit I needed?
Even if the picture succeeded commercially, as it probably would

because of Flynn, it certainly would not earn any critical acclaim or any satisfaction on my part. And how could I work on something when I wouldn't believe a word of what I was writing? It posed a basic question: could I function in Hollywood on terms that I could live with? It was risky, but I decided to put it to the test. "Dear Mr. Blanke, thank you for sending me the treatment. The subject matter is interesting but I'm afraid I don't like the story, at least in its present form."

Blanke must have been astonished by my rejection because he came rushing down to my office minutes after I sent the memo. Perhaps he was curious to see what kind of creditless idiot would turn down a Flynn picture. He was a bouncy man, very personable, with the capacity to muster tremendous enthusiasm for whatever film he was currently supervising.

"Why don't you like this story?"

"The chief reason, Mr. Blanke, is that I don't believe it."

"But you know Errol Flynn pictures. They're romantic adventures and that's what his audiences expect."

"I realize that, but I think his films might do even better if there were more substance, more credibility."

Blanke seemed somewhat impressed. "Well, Flynn says that too. He wants more of a character to play. What do you suggest?"

"I'd have to do some research, but I have a feeling that what actually happened with the privateers in that period might be more exciting than just another formula adventure story."

Blanke thought for a moment, then made his decision. "Go ahead. We'll see how it comes out."

The research department turned up some interesting historical facts about the English privateer Francis Drake during the reign of Queen Elizabeth. I decided to use him as a model for the Flynn role, although I was aware I'd have to take some liberties with history in romanticizing his career and particularly his love interest. What intrigued me was his relationship with the queen, played by Flora Robson, a superb actress who actually looked like the famous English monarch. The dominant military power in Elizabeth's time was Spain, whose wealth rested largely on exploiting the New World for its gold and silver, brought back to Spain in armed galleons. These were the ships that Drake and the other English privateers raided and plundered.

The politically astute Elizabeth was playing a double game. She very much wanted the crown's share of the plunder, but she was not ready militarily for a war with Spain. In response to the Spanish King Philip's angry protests, she claimed that the privateers were acting on their own and against her orders. But she did nothing to stop them. Her official rebukes of their piratical practices were for diplomatic purposes only, while she secretly admired and encouraged their exploits. This ambivalence in her position provided the basis for character-revealing scenes between the queen and Drake, who was perfectly aware of her approval and, at the same time, her need to disavow his actions to keep peace with Spain. In these scenes, wits, not swords, would be matched, counterpointing the physical violence of his encounters with the Spaniards in Panama and on the high seas.

My eventual script was approved by Blanke and especially welcomed by Errol Flynn, who was relieved to have a role that called for more than displaying his physical attributes. The son of a noted Australian anthropologist, Errol had enjoyed his share of real adventures in the South Seas early in his life. Now he wanted more than repeated travesties of the real thing on the screen. But he was incredibly handsome, and he did everything with grace, whether it was swordplay or lovemaking, and the studio had profited by exploiting these qualities.

I liked Errol from our first meeting. He had a reputation for wild parties and "womanizing," but that part of his life didn't concern me, although it was grist for the Hollywood gossip mills. Whatever his dissipations, they showed up neither in his appearance nor in the vitality he gave his performances—at least not until much later in his career.

During the time we worked together I found him open, friendly, amusing, and even somewhat sardonic about his "big star" position. Once we were talking on the set (Stage Seven, which was large enough for two huge ships, one English, the other Spanish, fully equipped and standing in real water with hundreds of extras as the crew and soldiers of both vessels) when Louella Parsons, the Hearst gossip columnist, came puffing up the ship's ladder to interview Errol. He muttered, "Christ, here she is again." Striding over to Louella, he grabbed her and swung her off her feet with such an excess of welcome that everyone, except possibly Louella herself, knew his extravagant gesture was satirical and that he didn't give a damn for her or her publicity.

At another time I could see that he was troubled with an up-coming scene, a close-up of him standing alone at the ship's rail getting his first glimpse of the Cliffs of Dover after one of his long privateering voyages away from home. All I had written for him in this shot was the single word "England . . ."

He came over to me. "Can't you give me something more to say than that—like, 'England, my home, and it's been so long,' or whatever."

"But, Errol, instead of a lot of words, I gave you those dots after 'England.' "

He looked puzzled. "Three dots. You want me to say, 'dot, dot, dot'?"

"I don't want you to say anything—just 'England.' The rest will be in your expression. You'll have a chance to act out your feelings."

He gave me an enigmatic smile. "But you see, I'm not an actor."

But he *was* an actor. He played that scene and those with Elizabeth sensitively and without losing their implications.

The director, Michael Curtiz, handled the difficult action scenes with expertise. The sea battles, the ambush of Drake in Panama, and the final swordplay between Drake and the traitorous Lord Wolfingham were all staged with the Curtiz flair for exciting visual movement. Mike and I had only one contretemps.

In the last scene, where Elizabeth is knighting Drake after the defeat of the Spanish Armada, I had the idea of making the queen's speech more stirring so that, when English audiences saw the picture, they would relate it to their present situation, faced with new invasion, this time from Nazi Germany.

I can't remember the lines I wanted to add, but whatever they were, Curtiz said, "No, no more words," and Blanke refused to interfere. Up to now I had gotten the scenes I'd wanted—and what Flynn wanted—into the film, and I should have dropped the argument. Foolhardily, I carried my appeal to the studio's highest court—Jack Warner himself. Probably he was only vaguely aware of me as an obscure, low-salaried writer whom Blanke, for some reason, had put on *The Sea Hawk*. His answer was immediate and typical: "Dear Koch, this picture is costing us a million and a half. If you want to buy it for an extra million above cost, you can put on any ending you please."

Not having that much change in my pocket, I couldn't take advantage of his offer. Too bad. Besides its favorable critical reception, it made the studio millions and is still earning money by its repeated showings on television.

However, other benefits stemmed from the picture's success. Up to now my secretaries kept changing while I noticed that each established writer had his own. Mine had to come from the secretarial pool because that was the custom for junior writers. Since I had broken one precedent by initially turning down the *Sea Hawk* treatment, and it had worked out well, I didn't see why I couldn't break another and have my own secretary. Besides, I had a particular girl in mind—the one who had been my very helpful (and attractive) assistant on the Mercury Theatre program back in New York.

With this intention I went to Walter MacEwen, head of the story department. He was slightly surprised by my request but thought it could be arranged. When I told him that the girl I wanted was not on the studio payroll and was, in fact, in New York, he was more than surprised. I explained that Anne Taylor would be an asset not only to me but to the studio, as she was bright and talented. For this reason I asked him to agree that, if

she worked out, Warners would eventually elevate her status—
and her salary.

By this time MacEwen was flabbergasted by my innocent presumption in making such an extraordinary request. Perhaps
innocent is the wrong word. No doubt he suspected that I wanted
Anne for more than secretarial purposes, and from his Hollywood
point of view, this put it all in a better light. It was their theory
that a happy writer was a good writer, and sex was considered an
important requisite to that desirable state. As it happened, his
suspicion was not quite justified. Our "love affair" remained pla-
tonic and our friendship has lasted to this day.

Again my unorthodox move brought the desired result. At the
end of her secretarial year Anne Taylor was working with me on
a screenplay for a film titled *Shining Victory*. The studio didn't
know about it, but Robert Lord, my producer on the picture, was
aware of it and approved. With his assistance I convinced Mac-
Ewen that she had earned a collaborative credit. The film received good notices and was a modest box-office success. From
then on, she was a writer on her own, both at Warners and later
at other studios.

John Huston, who was still looking after my interests, saw another possible benefit resulting from the success of *The Sea
Hawk*. He advised me to demand a new contract at a higher
salary. I thought my agent, Bill Dozier of the Berg, Allenberg
agency, was the proper one to make the request, but John said,
"No, have Berg himself do it. He has as much money as Warner
so Jack will listen to him."

John was right. After several months of negotiation and the
completion of another screenplay, my salary was doubled and
later tripled and quadrupled. But the most rewarding result was
my next assignment, which combined everything I could wish for
in its subject matter, its director, and its star.

THE LETTER

I could hardly believe my good fortune when another Warners producer, Robert Lord, sent me a Somerset Maugham short story, "The Letter," to dramatize for the screen. It was a psychological study of a woman who kills her lover and then uses all her imaginative resources to conceal the truth; eventually a letter sent her lover belies her plea of self-defense and she is destroyed. The story was set on a rubber plantation in Malaya, which provided the additional dimension of exotic locale.

Bette Davis, then at the peak of her brilliant career, was set to play the starring role, and William Wyler, at that time the most sought-after director in Hollywood, agreed to direct the picture. With this prize package for my second assignment I was back in paradise and more firmly entrenched. And the serpent had not yet put in its appearance.

Working with Willie Wyler was a valuable experience. He was
more visual than verbal, but after a while I was able to translate
his grunts, monosyllables, and facial expressions into approval or
disapproval. Wyler was a perfectionist, never letting go of a
scene until every possible dramatic value was milked to the last
drop. Even after the screenplay was marked "final" by the producer, I could tell from his troubled pacing of the floor that he
was still not completely satisfied. He tried to give me a clue to
what he felt was missing.

"Something . . . I don't know what . . . ought to remind
Bette of what she did . . . Not dialogue—some *thing*."

I puzzled over it for a day. What Wyler was searching for was
a fundamental image—something that by its recurrence would
reveal the woman's suppressed guilt behind the facade of her
protested innocence. Finally an idea came—nothing unusual, almost banal, but somehow it seemed appropriate.

"Willie, how about using the moon for the image you want?"

"Moon?"

"It's the tropics. Malaya. The night Bette shoots her lover there
could be a full moon that would flood the plantation. From then
on she could try to shut out the moonlight because of what it
recalls."

Willie nodded and began to devise the camera movements.
"OK, we'll track along the rubber trees. Stop on Bette. Smoking
gun in her hand. The lover lying dead at her feet in the moonlight. Then moon, moon, moon, every scene. Right?"

In the actual production Willie doubled the dramatic import
of my image. He used louvered blinds on the windows, which cut
the moonlight into stripes. Bette would try to keep out of its accusing light, but the moon would pursue her, printing prison
stripes on her dress. Willie never claimed to be an "auteur," as
do many directors today, but his interpretation of a writer's work
was creative, enhancing the values of the screenplay.

In the actual shooting he was equally meticulous. It was his
custom to do many takes of the same scene, earning him the

sobriquet "Twenty-Take Wyler," until he got exactly what he wanted in the can. Since production time is money, the front office, on viewing the daily rushes, would send him sharp warning memos: "If you don't speed up the shooting, you'll run over budget." Unimpressed, Willie would tear up the memo and continue at his own pace.

It was an unwritten law at Warners that a writer, once his script is marked "final," should stay off the set and go to work on his next project. To my delight Willie broke the rule for me. He insisted on my remaining with the company until he was certain that no line needed to be changed for any of the cast.

Among others, this brought me into daily contact with Bette Davis. During our first meeting in her mobile dressing room, I was overawed. She impressed me as a dormant volcano that could erupt into emotional flames at the slightest provocation. I suppose this is what is known as "star quality," making her the focal point for an audience when on screen. Fortunately she liked the part as written and had very few suggestions, so I was spared any collision on the set. She was raised in New England, I in upstate New York—common ground. By the end of shooting we had become friends, although on one occasion I came close enough to sparking an eruption that I could feel the heat. At the close of shooting a picture it was a Hollywood custom for those involved in the production to hold a farewell party. Usually it was the producer or director who gave it, but this time I invited the company to my place and Bette, of course, was the star guest.

Because we all felt so good about the film we had just made, I decided champagne was appropriate. With champagne, one bottle leads to another, and soon we were floating. From the patio where we held the party, Bette spied a croquet set on the lawn and wanted to play. We were not exactly in the best condition for a game of skill, but six of us picked up mallets and balls and the game started. At a certain point I hit Bette's ball. Since she was on the opposing side, I was ready to send her to hell and gone until out of the corner of my eye I saw her advancing on me with mallet raised. I doubt if she was serious, but after enough drinks, who knows? Anything can happen. I decided discretion was the better part of strategy and left her ball where it was, took my two shots, and came out of the game unscathed and, except for a hangover the next morning, none the worse for hosting my first Hollywood party.

A sidelight of the affair was Jack Warner's reported reaction. How he heard about it I have no idea, but the studio was a small world and as my secretary said, "Everybody knows everything here." His quoted remark was a typical Hollywood evaluation; "Where does a three-hundred-dollar-a-week writer get off giving a *champagne* party?" The answer, Mr. Warner, was that very shortly you were going to have to raise my salary to a level at which you felt champagne was appropriate.

My experience with a couple of early plays and the radio shows for Mercury taught me very little about acting as an art in itself. In my innocence all I asked of an actor was that he deliver the lines more or less as I had heard them in my mind as I wrote them. When *The Letter* company gathered in a semicircle facing Willie and me for the first reading of the script, I discovered how much more there was to acting than just giving back to the writer his own interpretation. I listened to Bette particularly, since she had the most dialogue. Suddenly I was aware of unexpected intonations in her reading that gave my lines new shades of meaning. I was happily conscious that I was getting back more than I had given.

It is a rare experience when there are no clashes of temperament, no serious disagreements or damaging compromises, among those involved in making a film. Somehow *The Letter* escaped these hazards and came through unscathed.

Perhaps the most important scene in any film is the ending, the impact of which the audience takes home. They may be stimulated by a sense of fulfillment, or they may be let down, no matter how effective the picture is up to that point. In the screenplay I had used the ending pretty much as Maugham wrote it—the woman, her guilt established, facing prison. Although it worked for the short story, the film needed something less prosaic and more dramatic. After the shooting was over, I wrote a new scene in which the ruined woman, in an act of expiation, walked out alone into the moonlit garden, knowing that the Oriental wife of the man she had murdered was waiting for her, knife in hand.

I took the new scene to Willie and he liked it. The shooting was over, the film in the can; but the set had not been struck and the two actresses we needed were still available. However, Hal Wallis, head of Warner production, would have to give his permission for us to do the retake scene.

Willie made an appointment to see Wallis and took me along to describe the new scene and its purpose. It was near noon on a Saturday morning, and Wallis was not in a receptive mood. He listened impatiently until I finished, then tried to dismiss us. "Sorry, no retakes. The picture's all right as it is."

Willie was not to be dimissed that easily. "But, Hal, if we can make it better, why shouldn't we?"

"We're already over budget."

"I can shoot the new scene in a day. And I'm off salary."

"The crew and the actors aren't." Wallis got to his feet. "Look, I'm going to Santa Anita and I'm late."

Willie didn't budge. "Just say 'yes,' Hal, and then go to the races." He grinned. "Although they'll probably cost you more than the retakes."

Wallis realized there was only one way to get rid of us. "Oh, Christ, go ahead, do the damn scene, but this picture had better make money."

It did and it still does. Bette played the new last scene with its tragic implications intact. The way Wyler directed it, the actual stabbing was left to the audience's imagination. As she walked out into the garden toward the avenging knife, a slight wind brushed her white scarf. The ghostly figure seemed to dissolve into the moonlight as though her dead lover had reclaimed her.

When I first saw the finished picture in a projection room, I found all I had envisioned when I wrote it, but vastly enriched by the contributing artists and craftsmen. The final judges of any film—the critics and the public—responded to its values, giving *The Letter* their unqualified approval. Later it was nominated for that year's Academy Award.

One exception. A friend of Wyler's sent him an amusing drawing of a rubber plantation with a half-dozen moons in the sky overhead. The only words were, "Why so much astronomy?" Willie laughed. "I guess I did shoot too many moons."

GIVE US THIS DAY
and
THE LONELY MAN

With the success of both *The Sea Hawk* and *The Letter*, my professional life was flourishing but my personal life was still like a badly constructed script, episodic, lacking emotional continuity. I had married very young. My wife, a talented art teacher, and I were separated. A conscientious mother, she and our two children were living in the East waiting for me to "grow up," as she put it with a great deal of justification. The children, Hardy and Karyl, twelve and nine years old but wise beyond those tender years, made gallant efforts to bridge the gap between their parents. Although I was devoted to them and enjoyed being with them when they visited, I was not yet ready for the responsibility of parenthood any more than I was for that of husbandhood. Then in my thirties, I was still sowing wild oats when I should have been harvesting them for possible literary use.

My current partner in dalliance was a young German-Jewish actress whom I shall call Kaisa. Among her attributes, which I then considered glamorous, was a taste for champagne, swimming pools, and the Hollywood night life, luxuries that had been denied her in Nazi Germany. With the help of friends she had escaped to this country, where Warners employed her as they did many refugees during this period. Because of her accent, appropriate roles were not easy to find despite an attractive, slim body, fawnlike eyes, and tawny hair blending with her perpetually suntanned skin. Exuding sex and inviting it up to a cutoff point, she contrived to remain technically a virgin. For what and for whom I have no idea.

It would be easy to say that extramarital affairs were indigenous to Hollywood and that I was simply caught up in its hedonistic life-style. Certainly the practice was common in the movie colony long before divorce became a national pastime. With the astronomical salaries this Hollywood period provided, life was lived on a lavish scale. Film people worked hard, but after hours they played just as hard. Romance flourished on and off the stages from Palm Springs to Malibu Beach. Many of my acquaintances, especially those of European background, were able to live what we call a double life without harming either partner, sometimes even to the enrichment of both. And some premarital sexual encounters can lead the way to the desired goal of a lasting relationship. However, I was not temperamentally adapted to keeping my experiences, marital and nonmarital, in separate compartments. Somewhere along the line they always collided, leaving in the wreckage a residue of guilt.

Actually my sexual adventures were a manifestation of a deeper problem, one I could trace back to a pre-Hollywood experience that followed the failure of my second Broadway play. I had attempted a drama on the subject of death, physical and spiritual, before I had learned very much about life. I had made such smooth transitions from parental care to academic and marital custody, all benevolent and protective, that at each new phase I was scarcely aware of any change. While I had encountered all manner of human miseries in my sociology forays with Dr. Edwards, those experiences were vicarious, happening to others, not to me. Intellectually they had informed me; emotionally I was not deeply involved.

My play's genesis was the funeral of my grandfather. I was twelve and it was my first contact with human death. He was a gentle, white-haired man who loved his large family and enjoyed listening to Strauss waltzes with his evening glass of beer. Having immigrated from Germany to avoid military conscription, he arrived just at the outbreak of our Civil War and, ironically, was almost immediately drafted into the Union Army and, according to family legend, was plunged into one of the bloodiest battles in history, Gettysburg. He survived and, as a small manufacturer, accumulated what was then a substantial fortune.

There came a day when I was called home from school, dressed in my Sunday suit, and taken to my grandparents' home in New York. Black crepe hung on the door, which was opened by solemn-faced relatives in dark, unfamiliar clothes, tiptoeing as though they were in church. It took all my courage to enter the darkened parlor, where I was told to pay my last respects to my grandfather. I began to cry, protesting that the wax effigy in the half-open coffin was not the grandfather I knew and loved. My outburst touched off a flood of tears among my relatives.

The funeral rites, held in a large hall, were designed to extract from the assembled mourners the full measure of their grief. I can still hear the muffled drums playing taps as the aging veterans of the Grand Army marched in slow step around the flag-draped casket. I can smell the banked lilies decaying in the heat of the crowded hall, an odor I still associate with death. At the cemetery I tried to shut my ears to the wailing of my relatives as the coffin was lowered into the earth. Afterward we all gathered in the cemetery restaurant. Unable to eat in spite of parental urging, I watched in bewilderment as the mourners, their tears hardly dried, ate voraciously, not understanding then that this was a natural reaction—an assertion of their aliveness in the wake of death.

I was also an unwilling spectator at the reading of the will. All the relatives had assembled in the parlor where the coffin had recently stood. The women were heavily veiled, the men wore black armbands. As the family lawyer opened the sealed document, I felt a suspense which at the time I couldn't analyze. I wanted to flee from that room to my upstate home.

The terms of my grandfather's will were simple. His fortune was left in equal shares to his children, to be distributed after the death of his widow, who was granted a life estate. At the time this seemed in keeping with my grandfather's strict sense of justice, but I sensed a disappointment among my elders and later I came to understand that a well-intentioned legacy may not necessarily be a wise one.

My grandmother was about sixty-five, lean of body and strong of will, who seemed in little danger of following her husband into an early grave. For the most part my relatives were kind people who would not wish harm to anyone. At the same time it was only natural that their attitude toward the person whose existence postponed their inheritance would have a certain ambivalence. My grandmother was so frugal she even saved the strings off grocery packages to sew into dishcloths. Her only luxuries were a glass of beer with her evening meal and subway trips to the cemetery every Sunday to put fresh flowers on my grandfather's grave. Consequently, she spent only a fraction of the income left her, but it never seemed to occur to her that she should share any of the accumulation with her children.

I remember we grandchildren were told to be "nice" to Grandma but I found her formidable and never knew what to say to her after the first greeting was over. Her thin gray hair was pulled back in a tight bun; her bony face was a deeply grooved relief map of her early hardships. Although sometimes she laughed, I can never remember her smiling. The only time her expression softened was when there was some mention of my grandfather. I saw my grandmother only at infrequent intervals, but as time went on, I began to sense something in her attitude close to defiance, a determination to remain on earth as long as possible if only to thwart those waiting for her demise. In fairness to her, she never demanded the anxious attentions showered on her, possibly aware that they were not entirely prompted by filial love.

Years passed and plans were deferred. New plans were made and these, too, had to be postponed. College educations for my cousins were given up for lack of funds. Families who wanted to move out of the city put it off until it was too late. Their children grew up and had children of their own. And the waiting was corroding their lives and crippling their ambitions. The present was being sold out, day by day, for a future that kept receding and eluding them. When finally the iron grip Grandma had on life relaxed, their lives and even the estate itself had shriveled. Most of the investments were in real estate in neighborhoods that had run down. The money that remained was duly divided among the aging children, but it couldn't restore the lost years or the lost hopes.

Here was a tragic theme, I told myself, worthy of an O'Neill or an Ibsen. With the audacity born of innocence I decided to make it the subject of my second play, building the action around the central situation and inventing composite characters that I hoped wouldn't be recognizable as any of my living relatives. In six months the first draft was finished, then came a second and some final polishing. The search for a title ended in an appropriate phrase from the Lord's Prayer, *Give Us This Day*. After only two or three submissions by my agent, a producer took an option on the play. Since I had been without income for nearly a year, the five-hundred-dollar advance was a godsend, and my hopes were soaring.

During the rehearsal period, however, some disturbing things began to happen. I was unhappy with the casting of the two leads, who were not characterized as I had envisioned them. My objections were shunted aside by the director, who was now in complete control. Then as the rehearsals progressed, I began to hear lines and even scenes that were not mine. Written by the director or some friend of his, they were slipped into the script without my being consulted. I protested to the Dramatists Guild, which tried to compromise our differences. I had the letter of the contract on my side, but I was an unknown playwright contesting the judgment of experienced professionals; there wasn't much I could do unless I was willing to take legal steps to stop the production. By the time we reached Philadelphia, where we were opening, I was completely isolated from my own play. The producer even asked me to stay away from the final rehearsals, claiming that my disapproving presence affected the work of the cast and director.

When the play opened to enthusiastic reviews from the Philadelphia critics, the producer and director took gleeful pleasure in pointing to the notices as proof that my pessimism was unjustified. Naturally wanting my play to succeed, I hoped they and the critics were right. But somehow, when I watched the performances, I couldn't convince myself. Superficially it "played," the story was well enough constructed, the serious scenes were counterpointed with comedy, the action built to theatrical climaxes, but something was missing, some element I couldn't define. I should have been moved by the tragic fate of my characters and I wasn't.

The critical reaction in New York bore out my worst fears, completely reversing the verdict in Philadelphia. I read every review with a kind of masochistic fascination. Except for the theme, which they agreed deserved better treatment, they had not a good word to say. Their sharpened pens ripped and slashed at the actors, the director, the set designer, and most of all, at me for my presumption in attacking a theme for which I was so inadequately equipped. With such notices no one dared go near the box office, and the play closed after two performances.

My reaction to the debacle was a strange one, and I don't fully understand it to this day. After the first numbing shock I suddenly experienced a kind of euphoria. I was happier than I'd been in months. I recall walking around the Central Park Reservoir with a sympathetic friend who couldn't fathom my mood and was even a little irritated by my perverse cheerfulness in the face of such a disaster. No doubt he thought I was pretending, but I wasn't. The October heavens never looked bluer, the skyline around the park seemed three-dimensional and majestic. I was intoxicated with the fall aroma of dried leaves and chestnuts roasting in a vendor's stand. It was as though my senses, dormant during the ordeal of the last month, had suddenly wakened to a new and heightened appreciation of the physical world. My friend looked at me, concerned that possibly the blow had unsettled my mind. I couldn't have explained it to him if I'd wanted to, but I didn't feel the need. I think I took some satisfaction in his perplexity.

From the perspective of the present the reasons for my euphoria are somewhat clearer. Partly, it was sheer relief from the tensions and unpleasantness of the rehearsal period. On a deeper level I realized that justice had been done, a harsh justice but one that gave me a new respect for my chosen life's work. The critics were right. Nor could I honestly blame the director or the cast or the changes in my script. Basically I was at fault. I had ventured in one foolhardy attempt to scale the highest peak of dramatic art before I was ready—and I had dropped into a crevasse. Up to then I'd resisted all discipline. Things had come easily, too easily and too early, but my facility had caught up with me. If I was to become a dramatist, I knew I would have to do a great deal of groundwork before trying again the steep ascent.

The first step was to analyze the reasons why *Give Us This Day* had fallen short of its ambitious goal. I had stumbled onto a fine theme—even the critics acknowledged that—and the central situation had an intrinsic dramatic tension. What was wrong? By elimination I came to the conclusion the fatal flaw was in the characters I had drawn more or less from life. I had not probed enough into their complex emotional states as they waited for their inheritance. I had oversimplified their motives and manipulated their behavior to fit the exigencies of the plot. The characters had a one-dimensional, theatrical life which might have been sufficient for melodrama, but they lacked a credible inner life with which the audience could identify and suffer and finally be purged—the requisites of tragedy.

This analysis led me to another conclusion which wasn't easy to face and which, for a time, I resisted. The fault lay not so much with my craft as with my lopsided development as a person. On a surface level I got along well enough with people, but in my egocentric world they were little more than supporting players to the leading role I had assigned myself. Abstractly I desired a better world for humanity and was even willing to work for it, but I had not yet developed the capacity to feel deeply for a single human being.

Naturally I couldn't articulate this as lucidly as I can in retrospect, but at least the *Give Us This Day* experience had jolted me into some awareness of my immaturity. Since psychological surveys have borne evidence that a retarded emotional development is prevalent among American males, I could take some comfort that my condition was neither extraordinary nor incurable. But a dramatist has to understand people and the obvious prerequisite is that he understand himself.

The question presented itself—how does one hasten the process of "growing up" so as to come into self-knowledge and a compassionate understanding of the behavior of others? Evidently it wasn't something you could acquire from books or lectures or the advice of well-intentioned friends. The conclusion was obvious: you learn about life from living.

The result of my self-analysis led me down some strange byways. In my impatience to make up for lost time, I took some drastic measures in the naive notion that I could put myself in a sort of pressure cooker to bring my laggard emotions to a quick boil. I realize this may have been a late reaction to the failure of my play, steeping myself in new sensations to get over the after-effects of a serious blow to my ego.

At this time I met a girl I shall call Amy Peterson. Her family—sister, brother, mother, and her mother's lover, all handsome, vital people—lived a gypsy's life. For part of the year they squatted, rent-free, in a ramshackle house in the mountains above Woodstock. The winter I met them they were camping in a two-room flat in Greenwich Village. I say "camping" because they never seemed permanent anywhere. They had few possessions, scarcely any furniture, a washtub for bathing, and one bed which the mother shared with her lover while the children unrolled their sleeping bags wherever they found enough space on the floor. However, if one of the children brought home a lover, the grown-ups obligingly gave up their bed, taking their turn on the floor so that the young couple could sleep together in reasonable comfort and privacy.

In spite of their grimy, cluttered quarters, they always managed to look neat and attractive in homemade clothes which they wore with a certain flair. Each had a different art, except Mrs. Peterson's boyfriend, who worked at journalism when he worked at all. Amy, haunting the junk shops, became an authority on antique furniture, which she occasionally bought and sold. Her mother was a sculptress, her sister painted, and her brother was skilled at various handicrafts. While each maintained a certain independence, they shared with each other not only the bed but whatever else they had, including any money that came their way, suggesting that a collective life doesn't necessarily mean a sacrifice of individuality. The Petersons may have been among the last of the bohemians in the Greenwich Village tradition of the Millay sisters, John Reed, and Max Bodenheim.

In my rebellious state, searching for something I couldn't define, the Petersons had an enormous appeal, especially Amy. They blithely disregarded all the conventional rules I had been brought up to consider sacred. Most of the people I knew were tied to a

job, a school, a house, or a marriage. The Petersons were tied to
nothing. Like migrating birds, they moved as the seasons and
their instincts dictated. Observing their casual way of living, so
alien to my own, I was intrigued but not quite able to shed my
past upbringing and meet them on their own terms.

Although I had very little money, compared to the Petersons I
was affluent. I could afford to take Amy to a show or dinner at a
restaurant, which she enjoyed in the way a tourist might take
pleasure in a foreign scene. We had some things in common,
among them radical attitudes in politics, but I think what most
attracted us to each other was our different life-styles.

At this time I was still married to Lucie and by my standards
these excursions with Amy were strictly illicit. But she couldn't
have cared less whether I was single or had ten wives. She had
no designs on me of any permanent nature. It was enough that
at the moment I wanted to be with her and she with me. Or if I
no longer cared to take her out, that was all right too. She simply
had no sense of what was beginning to trouble my conscience.

A relationship such as ours couldn't remain static. It had either
to deepen or to deteriorate, and the only way it could deepen was
in sexual consummation. Amy was not promiscuous; she was
merely responsive to what she felt. After an evening together,
pausing at her front door, she looked at me questioningly. "Coming up?"

Sooner or later I knew I would be faced with a decision. Either
I would have to burn my Victorian bridges or give Amy up. She
was desirable and I wanted her. While Amy waited for an answer, my imagination pictured what was ahead if I accepted her
invitation.

First of all, the bed—that busy bed. Whoever was in it would
quickly vacate in our favor, since the rules of the house prescribed that it should go to whoever could make the best use of
it on the particular night. And the Petersons were all agreed that
love took precedence over sleeping. Amy would give a signal and
we would tiptoe around the bodies on the floor and occupy the

bed. For however long we wanted, it would become an island cut off from the mainland of what I conceived to be my real life.

But inevitably morning would come. The seas of passion would recede and the island would rejoin the mainland. I would go back home. Questions would be asked. Questions had already been asked. This time there would be only one answer, "Yes, I was unfaithful."

My wife was charitable in many areas but extramarital sex was not one of them. Raised in the Middle West Bible Belt, she had a strict moral code. Although she had studied in art school and associated with artists, by temperament she was a teacher and a very good one. She was also mature but had the misfortune of having married someone who wasn't.

I never occupied the Peterson family bed. Mrs. Peterson, honestly concerned about my sex life, paid a friendly visit to my wife to discuss what could be done about it. I wasn't present so I don't know what happened, but with two women so polarized in their sexual mores, it must have been a very interesting meeting.

My marriage survived the incident, at least in a formal sense, but the erosion had begun, and in spite of good intentions on both sides, there was no reversing the process. Another two years passed before we were willing to acknowledge the inevitable. As for Amy, we still saw each other but less and less. By her own admission she had taken a lover. Like Nina in *Strange Interlude*, she was able to divide her social and sexual needs; unlike Nina, she was not neurotic but adjusted to what under the circumstances seemed practical. Naturally, the arrangement pleased me less than it did her, although I realized I was at fault. The last I heard of Amy she had married a titled Englishman and lived in a manor house in Kent, no doubt furnished in the antiques she loved. I hope her husband enjoyed her as much as I did and received as good an education in some of the arts of living.

By then a definite character pattern was emerging which I was resolved to break. I had gone to college too soon, married too young, practiced law before I was equipped, written a serious play prematurely, and had my first affair before I could make a complete relationship.

For six months during my involvement with Amy, I had put aside my writing in the belief that first I must do more living. While every experience is important to a writer if he is able to appraise it objectively, I was beginning to realize the futility of trying to track down "life" like a hunter. Sooner or later it comes to all of us, sometimes in ways we don't recognize or appreciate. The experiences most meaningful and useful often come in the disguises of our losses and failures. From these I was no longer immune.

My next play on a social theme was more within the scope of my abilities at this stage in my career. It was *The Lonely Man,* which led me to the Mercury Theatre, which in turn eventually opened the way to Hollywood.

The severe depression of the early thirties touched off a trend in social plays. The Group Theatre, with Clifford Odets as its resident playwright, was flourishing on the New York stage. The Federal Theatre, supervised by Hallie Flanagan and Elmer Rice, introduced *The Living Newspaper* as a new theatrical form to Broadway, dealing with contemporary problems in documentary fashion. Regional theatres, funded by the New Deal, sprang up all over the country. In the theatre, people seemed to be finding an escape from the pressure of their daily problems or, possibly, reassurance that certain values transcended and survived their economic plight.

The twenties had been marked by wild stock market speculation. Success was measured in monetary terms, with the Dow Jones charts its barometer. When the market crashed, so did many of our illusions. With the election of President Roosevelt, the nation began to repair the ravages of the twenties. New values were asserting themselves: art, education, the protection of our resources, human and natural. In this galvanized atmosphere it was natural for me to write a play reflecting the national mood. *The Lonely Man* was based on a fantastic premise, the return of young Lincoln to our contemporary world to find that slavery still existed, but in other forms. His struggle to extend the concept of freedom to all races and all segments of our society was the conflict of the play.

An option was taken by Robert Milton, a talented man with pink hair who had just directed another fantasy, *Outward Bound,* with considerable success. The main problem we faced was to find a young actor with the authority to play the Lincoln character. Together we went through casting lists but could find no one we thought was right.

One day during a torrential rainstorm a tall young man appeared at the door of my New York apartment, sent by Robert Milton. Hatless, disdaining umbrella or raincoat, water still dripping from his unruly black hair, he burst into our West Side apartment as though driven by the wind. He had no training and practically no experience as an actor, but he had crowded almost everything else into his thirty years, including writing a version of *Frankie and Johnny,* painting, prizefighting, and bumming around Europe as an itinerant artist and adventurer. None of this mattered. After fifteen minutes I knew he was heaven-sent for the role of young Lincoln, a gift of Pluto, the god of storms. The young man was John Huston.

The Lonely Man opened at the Blackstone Theatre in Chicago under the joint auspices of Robert Milton and the Federal Theatre. There have been many Lincolns on the stage and screen, some very good ones, but I believe John's characterization stands out as the most penetrating. He used none of the usual makeup—no beard, no stovepipe hat, no drawl. He *thought* Lincoln with a brooding intensity that came over the footlights with such conviction that the audiences were mesmerized into accepting the story's fantastic premise. In spite of our last-minute revisions, my play still had many flaws and was not up to its theme, but it served the purpose of providing a vehicle for John's tour de force. Hailed by critics and Lincoln scholars, people came from all over the country to see his performance and the play ran for a season.

Two persons who traveled considerable distances to watch John perform were his elderly grandmother and his father, Walter Huston, himself one of the finest actors of our time. Until then John and his father had not seen much of each other. Perhaps Walter had partly written off his erratic son as a ne'er-do-well. John's achievement in Chicago evidently opened Walter's eyes to his son's potential. From then on their film careers paralleled and finally merged in the superb *Treasure of the Sierra Madre*, in which John directed his father in his Oscar-winning perform-ance. Their close personal relationship continued until Walter's sudden death after they had dined together one night in Beverly Hills. At his funeral, I remember John's moving tribute: "My father was too big a man to get sick; when his time came, he just died."

As for Gram, as John called his grandmother, she sat in the first row every night of his performance. His exit after the first scene always brought a round of applause from the audience. One night for some reason the applause didn't come. This was an omission Gram refused to brook. With the help of her cane, she struggled to her feet, faced the audience with a stern expression, and stopped the show while she clapped her hands until the others joined in. Of all the tributes, I think this is the one John enjoyed the most.

During our stay in Chicago, I saw a great deal of John and gained some insight into other sides of his complex personality. To his friends he was extravagantly generous, but if anyone dis-pleased him, he could be withering and sadistic, as in his re-lationship with Montgomery Clift, the talented star then sick and drug-ridden and near the end of his brilliant career. Enormously creative, John was also destructive, both of himself and of others.

When he gave you his attention, it was total. You alone existed for him, but only as long as he could draw out of you what of immediate interest you had to give, then, in movie terms, fade out and fade in to whatever next claimed his probing concentration. Once you understood this and accepted him on his own terms, you could remain his friend. However, with women—well, proceed at your own risk. Many were drawn into the magnetic field of his sexuality; few escaped without some scars.

One day during rehearsals in Chicago we were walking through the lobby of the Palmer House when a couple passed, a beautiful woman with a slightly older man. The man was speaking to her in French. John stopped and followed the couple with his eyes as they made their way to the bar. With no more explanation than "His French accent's phony," he strolled into the bar while I waited outside, curious to see what he was going to do. John appropriated an empty stool next to the girl, and in a few minutes he also appropriated the girl, to the intense annoyance of her escort. I could see her gradually shift her attention from him to the absorbing stranger on her left. After a round of drinks she said a brief word to her escort, rose, and walked off with John. The other man was forgotten. I was forgotten. For one night the girl would have all of John's fierce attention and after that, nothing. The next day when I asked about his conquest, he had already dismissed her from his mind.

Yet there was a yearning in John for a more stable relationship, perhaps stimulated at the moment by his success in the play and his father's approval. A young Englishwoman by the name of Leslie Black, attractive, intelligent, cultivated, was traveling around the world, recovering from a brief and unhappy marriage. She came to the play as Robert Milton's guest, met John, and there her journey ended. John left Chicago that fall, the play closed, and he and Leslie were married. The next five years, while John was building their California home and his film career, were perhaps the high point of both their lives.

But once he had attained what he wanted, his restless nature demanded new stimulations. And they were all too available as far as women were concerned. His work brought him into daily contact with actresses attached to the studio, many of them exciting and beautiful women. This time John didn't take his dilemma lightly. One morning he came to my office as troubled as I ever remember him. He put his problem bluntly. He still loved Leslie but he was *in* love with one of the stars in the film he was directing—and they were having an affair.

I had nothing much to offer except some understanding of his divided loyalties. Although I didn't have John's backlog of such situations, I was soon to face a similar decision, so I certainly couldn't preach morality to him. Moreover, I knew John well enough by now to foresee that all his life he would be using up people and places, sucking them dry of whatever interested him, and then moving on to the next and the next and the next.

The restless adventurer and the creative artist seemed to alternate in different phases of his life, and the films he eventually directed reflected this dichotomy in their varying quality from mediocre to great. The adventurous side of his nature was reflected in his need to gamble. Symbolically, his next marriage, this time to the actress Evelyn Keyes, took place in Las Vegas. With gambling, it wasn't only cash he laid on the line; often it was his life. Whether it was playing Russian roulette—which he played with Mexican cavalry officers, tossing loaded pistols in the air to see whose body would receive the chance bullet—or hunting elephants on the African veldt or riding to hounds on his Irish estate, John courted danger. He talked very little of his early life, but one story he told me seemed revelatory. When he was a young boy, his divorced parents had put him in a Texas school where he was unhappy and sickly. One night he made up his mind to settle the issue of whether to live or die. He slipped out of the dormitory and, stripping off his clothes, lay all night in the icy water of a nearby mountain stream. If he survived the ordeal of pneumonia, he would prove to himself that he possessed the physical and mental resources to overcome the ill health and loneliness that plagued his boyhood years. He would either die or live fully.

On one occasion we got on the subject of death. More as an exercise in logic, I suggested that the law of conservation of energy might apply to consciousness (whatever and wherever that is), as well as to matter, and might, in some form, persist after death. The thought startled John. As some take comfort in a possible afterlife, his ultimate desire was oblivion, to be erased from conscious existence. When he was planning his attractive home in the San Fernando Valley, he wanted it built of materials that would crumble and return to the earth after he and Leslie were through with it. Permanence of any kind was anathema.

Why? Everyone who knew John well or slightly—and they were legion—had some theory about him. He had been born with a death wish, or the opposite, that he feared death and had to defy it to prove that he was not afraid. Or, like his friend Hemingway, he needed constantly to demonstrate his virility. Any or all of these may be part of the truth. My own feeling is that John's *bête noire* was boredom. Like an opium eater who saw his supply running out, John dreaded outliving those things that gave his life the stimulation he craved—a mountain he hadn't scaled, a wild beast he hadn't shot, a woman who could offer him a new sexual challenge. It seemed to me that he kept death within easy reach as a sort of ace in the hole against boredom, to be played at any time he had exhausted what the world had to offer.

I don't see John anymore. Our paths have diverged. But I shall always remember with respect and affection the tall, intense, Lincolnesque figure who appeared out of a storm, a lonely man who for a time held us all in his spell.

SERGEANT YORK

FADE IN

INT. OFFICE WRITERS' BUILDING WARNERS STUDIO

DAY

The time is 1943.

CLOSE-UP TITLE PAGE

of a sheaf of papers lying on a desk. Across the front page is written the typed words:

SERGEANT YORK

A Treatment

CAMERA PULLS BACK to reveal H.K. seated at his desk. Across from him is JOHN HUSTON, one lanky leg stretched over a corner of the desk. H.K. is talking while HUSTON sketches him with vigorous pencil strokes on a drawing pad held in his lap. H.K. appears a little self-conscious.

H.K.

John, you listening?

HUSTON

(*nods*)
Go on, go on.

H.K.

(*indicating the treatment*)
This is a pro-war picture, you know that?

(*Huston looks up, seems to be studying* H.K., *then back to his sketching before he answers.*)

HUSTON

Well, we're in a war.

This was the answer, of course. With the country now deeply involved in World War II, the Warners were anxious to make *Sergeant York* as a morale builder and a picture expected to profit from its timeliness. The question I raised with Huston was a reminder that our previous collaboration had been on a stage play titled *In Time to Come* whose subject was peace through collective security, dealing with the tragedy of Woodrow Wilson and the ill-fated League of Nations.

Before coming to Hollywood I had written an early version of *In Time to Come*. In Chicago I discovered that John was thinking of a play on the same subject. We decided to pool our efforts, using my first draft as a starting point. After long discussions in Chicago and later in Hollywood, I wrote a second draft to which John added many ideas that enhanced its theatricality. By 1941 we had the finished play, which Otto Preminger produced and directed late in that year.

The reviews of the New York critics were glowing, with a special blessing from Brooks Atkinson of *The New York Times*, then the dean of the drama critics. Everyone foresaw a long run but as it turned out, our timing of a peace play was somewhat off. Pearl Harbor intervened, and the country's preoccupation was not on the prevention of war but on its prosecution; after six struggling weeks, the play closed.

In the play, as in his life, Wilson warned those who opposed him that without American participation, the League would be ineffectual and a second world war inevitable. This was hardly a prophecy we wished to see fulfilled, but here we were working on a film about this next world war.

Jesse Lasky, one of the early Hollywood tycoons, had lost his own studio during the depression and was now employed as a producer at Warners. In his comeback effort he had secured the rights to do a film on the life and exploits of Alvin York, whose single-handed capture of a whole German company had made him the most publicized hero of World War I.

This was my first experience working directly with another writer. John let me do most of the talking while he sketched. Occasionally I couldn't resist stealing a glance at my portrait to see if he was doing me justice or, better still, improving on the original. If some idea of mine struck John as useful, he would stop his sketching and often improvise the action for a whole scene.

Lasky, a gentle, soft-spoken man with no creative pretensions, left us pretty much to our own resources. We soon realized that York's actual life, at least up to his famous war exploit, was not very dramatic. So we took extravagant liberties with his backwoods rearing and his courtship of a neighbor girl. We exaggerated his hell-raising for dramatic contrast with his religious family background. Perhaps the most amusing scene in the picture turned out to be a contrived incident leading to his conversion. Returning, on muleback, from a hard-cider spree with his buddies, he is struck by a bolt of lightning and knocked off his mule. Taking this as a warning from heaven, Alvin appears unexpectedly at a rural church service, joining the delighted congregation in a lively rendition of "That Old-Time Religion." How the real Alvin York felt about the flamboyant version of his religious conversion I never heard. But he did give the film his approval and made a personal appearance at its opening.

The screenplay finished, John left for a project of his own which was to become his first directorial assignment.

Again I was fortunate in the choice of our director. Howard Hawks, who had made a number of distinguished films, left the screenplay pretty much to the writers but worked closely with the actors. In contrast to Mike Curtiz, his manner was relaxed, restrained, unhurried. I never heard him raise his voice. When he wanted to convey or correct an interpretation of some role, he would draw the actor aside to make his suggestion in private. Many Hollywood directors and producers seemed to have no life other than their current movie. But Hawks kept his private and professional lives apart. He gave me the impression of a cultured gentleman at home in both worlds. Politically he was closer to John Wayne's position than to mine, but we never discussed politics. Our relationship was strictly professional.

Gary Cooper was ideal casting for the central role of a mountaineer character, a lanky outdoor man with a winning simplicity combined with Yankee shrewdness. In keeping with the Alvin York character he was playing, Cooper was somewhat taciturn on and off the screen, and communication was not easy unless it was on the subject of hunting or some other outdoor sport. I remember our first "talk" on the set the day shooting began.

"Any suggestions, Mr. Cooper? Lines you're not comfortable with?"

"Nope."

"You've read through the script?"

"Yup."

"And you want nothing changed?"

"Nope."

"Well, to a writer those are kir·d words."

He gave me a warm, understanding smile. I was making progress. If I could just get him past monosyllables.

"You met the real Sergeant York?"

"Yup."

"What did you think?"

"That man can sure shoot."

I had no interest in shooting—turkeys or Germans. Apparently York was adept at both and our turkey-shoot scene in the picture was legitimate.

Lasky and Warners had guessed right—*Sergeant York* became the biggest box-office success of that period. I saw it recently on television and I was less favorably impressed than at the time it was made. The pivotal scene was York's inner struggle to reconcile his newfound religion with his patriotic duty to fight for his country. The commandment "Thou shalt not kill" was in direct conflict with his participation in an endeavor whose purpose was to kill. In an attempt to dramatize this subjective process we had York (Cooper) spend a day alone on a mountaintop trying to resolve the dilemma. Since his decision to go to war was a matter of history, we had York find his solution in Christ's words as written in the New Testament: "Render unto Caesar what is Caesar's and unto God what is God's."

Our resolution worked well enough for that time and under those circumstances. But appraising it from today's perspective, the biblical quotation seems less convincing. If you render unto all the Caesars, past and present, what they demand of us, there is little left for God. They get what they want—power, glory, money, or whatever—and He comes out on the short end.

Finished with *Sergeant York*, I was assigned to collaborate with the Epstein brothers on what turned out to be, despite its complicated origin, a film that made cinema history—*Casablanca*.

CASABLANCA

Now in its third decade, *Casablanca* shows little sign of aging or diminishing in popularity. Since its original release it has played more revival dates than any other film in motion picture history, in both 35- and 16-millimeter. Although it is not an art film in the usual sense, it is shown consistently in art and university theatres over the country. More articles have been written about it than any other picture with the possible exception of *Citizen Kane*. At the University of Illinois it was the subject of a thesis for a master's degree. "Rick's Place" was used as a military code for the city of Casablanca in World War II. Restaurants and nightclubs in many cities have been named for the film, and one in Philadelphia has actually duplicated the set of Rick's Café Américain. Dialogue and stills from the movie are used in periodicals to advertise various products. The title of the Broadway film by Woody Allen, *Play It Again, Sam*, needed no footnote to explain its origin. Everyone knew it was from *Casablanca*, even though the actual words in the movie were "Play it, Sam." No doubt the "again" simply underlined the average person's nostalgic memory of the scene in which Bogart sits drinking in the closed café while Dooley Wilson sings "As Time Goes By."

For whatever reason, *Casablanca* has worked its way past its movie origins and into our language. Yet none of us involved in its production could have foretold that it was to have an illustrious future or, in fact, any future at all. Conceived in sin and born in travail, it survived its precarious origin by some fortuitous combination of circumstances to become the hardiest of Hollywood perennials, as tough and durable as its antihero, Humphrey Bogart.

It all began when Warners purchased the movie rights to an unproduced play by Murray Burnett and Jean Alison entitled *Everybody Comes to Rick's*. Although I didn't come on the assignment until much later, stories of its early vicissitudes filtered down to me. It seems that Jack Warner bought the rights to the play with the idea of making another *Algiers*, a very successful film set in the same exotic locale. The practice of seeking to duplicate or remake previous hits has plagued the industry from its early days and, unfortunately, is still prevalent. For the leads in the *Neo-Algiers* Mr. Warner had in mind George Raft and Hedy Lamarr. However, Raft turned down the role, and *Casablanca* narrowly escaped the Casbah.

At this point the casting took a ninety-degree turn. The new selections were less bizarre but hardly more distinguished—Dennis Morgan for Rick, Ann Sheridan for Ilsa, and—believe it or not—Ronald Reagan for Laszlo, the idealistic antifascist leader. For whatever reason, the casting wheel took another spin and this time stopped at the lucky number—Humphrey Bogart, Ingrid Bergman, Paul Henreid, Claude Rains, Peter Lorre, and a superb supporting cast, all identified with *Casablanca* in such a way that it would be difficult to imagine other actors in any of the roles.

After passing through various hands, the assignment for the screenplay came to Julius and Philip Epstein, two very accomplished and witty screenwriters who deservedly received first credit on the finished film. Under the best circumstances, writing for the screen is a hazardous occupation. In this instance the Epsteins were faced with the additional problem of adjusting to the casting gyrations. While most of the roles were finally filled by studio contract players, Jack Warner and Hal Wallis, the film's producer, wanted a new face for the female lead. Their selection of Ingrid Bergman, a Swedish actress then beginning her Hollywood career, turned out to be a felicitous choice. She possessed the personal qualities needed to portray the romantic idealist with conviction and without sentimentality, and her slight accent lent authenticity to the character's middle-European background.

At the time Miss Bergman was "owned" by David Selznick under the terms of a long contract and could be pried away only by the lure of a good story that would advance her career and her box-office value to the Selznick organization. In the words of Julius Epstein: "Jack Warner summoned my brother and me and said we had to go to Selznick and talk him into letting us have Bergman and that David would want to know every detail of the screenplay. We said we didn't know what to say, but Warner told us to make up something, anything, just bring back Bergman. Phil and I were ushered into Selznick's office and I got things started by saying it was a romantic melodrama with a sinister atmosphere. Dark lighting and a lot of smoke . . . Selznick slapped the desk top and said, 'That's all I need to know, you've got Bergman.' "

By this time events connected with the war had begun to influence the shape and direction of the story. The idea of making another *Algiers* was discarded for more current and relevant elements.

While these decisions were being made, the Warner time clock was ticking away. As was often the custom in such situations, the front office decided to assign an additional writer, and I was asked to collaborate with the Epsteins. All I knew at the time was that the projected film, initiated by a play I had not read, was to be called *Casablanca,* with a talented action director, Michael Curtiz, and an imposing cast waiting in the wings.

My collaboration with the Epsteins was entertaining and productive but short-lived—they were called to Washington on a war service project. The morning I heard the news was not one of my happiest moments. In the movie world there is no substitute for success and no acceptable excuse for failure. I had inherited from the Epsteins excellent material, some in sequence, some not, which I assumed contained what was useful from previous Warner efforts and from the original play. However, there was still much work to be done before we had a final script, approved for shooting. With the production deadline creeping up and with Mike Curtiz importuning me for pages that could be mimeographed and sent around to the various departments, I felt under more pressure than on any previous assignment.

The opening sequence served to establish the wartime atmosphere of Casablanca. From their research my predecessors had devised some lively incidents that evoked the period and place. Casablanca was a Moslem city and during the Second World War was a way station for refugees fleeing German-occupied Europe to neutral countries. It was notoriously corrupt. There was little distinction between the Vichy authorities who were supposed to enforce the laws and the criminals who made money by breaking them, both sides working profitably together. As in Saigon of the sixties, anything could be bought and sold on the black market—foreign currency, jewels, visas, girls, even human lives.

This montage set the stage for the initial dramatic incident—the reported murder of the two German couriers which put in

motion the chain of events in a story by now so familiar it is unnecessary to detail them. For the uninitiated, the screenplay is
included in various film anthologies.

To the extent that I influenced the film's direction, it was in the
emphasis on the political elements. The most provocative relationship in the story was that between Rick (Bogart) and Captain Renault (Claude Rains) because it was ambiguous and its
denouement unpredictable. The resolution of their relationship
was closely tied in to the fate of Ilsa (Bergman) and the antifascist leader, Laszlo (Henreid). For this reason I concentrated
on the cat-and-mouse game between Rick and the French pre-
fect, cutting down to a large extent Renault's seductive pursuit
of the refugee girl, Anina.

A few weeks from the shooting date I recall taking stock of
where we were, the "we," of course, including the collective work
of myself and the others who had preceded me. Numerically we
had about sixty pages, about one-half of the screenplay. They
were sent to Curtiz, who responded with enthusiasm although I
think Mike was so worried and hungry for script that any pages
marked "final" would have looked good to him.

In the meantime the cast grew aware that there was no finished
script since they were getting it in pieces. To most of them this
was not an unfamiliar situation and, with the exception of Ingrid
Bergman, they were probably less concerned than the director
and I. Miss Bergman, not yet inured to the ways of Hollywood,
showed some signs of unease and with good reason. At this point
she didn't know (nor did we) whether she was going to end up
with Bogart or with Henreid. The question was resolved in favor
of an ending in keeping with the political convictions of the
characters rather than the conventional leading-man-gets-leading-
lady resolution. If the latter had been adopted, I believe *Casablanca* might still have been an entertaining melodrama but certainly not one with its special and lasting appeal.

Bogart, true to the role he played, kept his "cool." On occasion
he would invite me into his dressing room with his usual, "Relax

and have a drink." We would talk and sometimes an idea or a line of dialogue would pop out of the whiskey bottle.

As the camera began catching up with the script, a memo arrived from the front office with the reminder that any day in which the director had no scenes to shoot would cost the studio thirty thousand dollars—a warning that didn't add to my peace of mind.

At the same time new complications developed. During the initial stages Curtiz was so relieved to see pages accumulating that he accepted them without reservation or with slight modifications. However, as the screenplay began to take its final shape, Mike was assailed by second thoughts and doubts. Accustomed to success on a certain level, he dreaded the possibility of a box-office failure.

In this uncertain state of mind, he did what was so often the practice of producers and directors. He started giving out the incomplete script to various colleagues on the lot. Inevitably, their reactions varied, and Mike's attitude toward the story shifted with the changing winds. When I protested that some of the suggested changes were illogical and out of character, he would answer impatiently in his Hungarian idiom, "Don't worry what's logical. I make it go so fast no one notices."

As the distance between script and shooting narrowed and the pressures increased, our disagreements erupted into quarrels. Despite the multiplicity of writers working in relays—usually fatal to any dramatic work—I felt that a certain unity had been achieved that could easily be destroyed by tampering with the emerging script. Mike, on his part, felt that his directorial prerogatives were being challenged by a writer who was supposed to make his contribution and then conveniently disappear.

From my present perspective I can be more objective. I realize the difference between us was mostly a matter of emphasis. Mike leaned strongly on the romantic elements while I was more interested in the characterizations and the political intrigues with their relevance to the struggle against fascism. Surprisingly, these disparate approaches meshed, and perhaps it was partly this tug-of-war that gave the film a certain balance.

One disagreement I remember arose over the flashback sequence in which Rick recalls his Paris love affair with Ilsa. I argued that these could only be conventional scenes with no dramatic progression until the end shot when Ilsa fails to show up at the railroad station. While they illustrated the cause of Rick's bitterness and cynicism, I felt these were sufficiently exposed in the café scene with Ilsa. I was afraid that the flashback would dissipate the tension that was building in the present.

In retrospect I suspect Mike was right. At this point the romantic interlude was a useful retard and relief from tension. Also, the viewer needed some visual proof of the ardor of the love affair to be convinced of its profound effect on Rick. At any rate, Mike exercised his directorial prerogative and the sequence was written and shot in accordance with his ideas.

The final weeks were a nightmare of which I remember only fragments. During this part of the shooting, revised pages started coming through mimeograph from sources unknown to me. Later I learned that the Epsteins, having returned from Washington, had rejoined the project. Even though we were working independently, our contributions must have meshed, with results beneficial to the picture. When it was all over and the words *Fade Out. The End* had been typed on the much-revised and multi-authored script, I had only the foggiest notion of what sort of film would emerge from the composite of our efforts. In January 1943, when the film opened at Warners' Hollywood Theatre, I wondered what all the excitement was about. I was still blind to the virtues of the picture and saw only what I considered its faults. When a year later it received the Academy Award, I was by that time inured to miracles.

We can admit without excess modesty that there have been more profound films than *Casablanca*. On close examination one can find elements that are inconsistent and illogical. Judged as a realistic picture of political events in North Africa, it would fall short of a film such as *The Battle of Algiers*. Moreover, in these times when each action movie tries to outdo its predecessor in brutality and bloodletting, *Casablanca* is curiously lacking in overt violence. In only three scenes is there any gunplay, and these are brief and understated. Most of the tension derives from dangers implicit in the situations and atmosphere, and much of the conflict is in the realm of ideas. It would seem that the film retains its popularity not because it conforms to the contemporary mood but in spite of it. What then is there about *Casablanca* that continues to inspire the affection and loyalty of so many people?

There are almost as many reasons given for its durability as there are critics, columnists, and movie buffs who have tried to analyze it. Some have discovered overtones and reverberations in the film of which I, at least, was not conscious. Among the younger generations a sort of mystique has grown up around the film and its protagonist, Bogart. Students tell me of *Casablanca* clubs in some colleges whose members are expected to attend a performance each time it is revived in their area. Some have reported seeing it as many as fifteen times. At Harvard, where I was told it is shown twice a year, it has become a sort of ritual, with the audience speaking the lines in chorus along with the actors. When I took part in a student seminar at Stanford, I asked why this impassioned loyalty to a movie made over a quarter of a century ago? One of the students, Walter Bougere, volunteered to interview young people in the Stanford community to find out their answers to my question.

Reading their comments, I was struck by their consistency—different words, but the same trend of thought about the film and its significance to them. Perhaps in reacting to a fictional world, these students could more easily expose their feelings about the real world as they find it today when right and wrong can't be as clearly defined as it is in *Casablanca*.

I was moved by their comments because they revealed a latent idealism under the protective mask of cynicism, much like the tough-tender stance of Bogart's Rick in the film. However, the times and the political circumstances now are as different as World War II was from Vietnam. In the end Rick found an outlet for his repressed idealism, something worth a personal commitment and sacrifice. They can't, or at least haven't up to now, and our world is the worse for providing no comparable moral equivalent. One student summed up their feelings about the film in this way: "*Casablanca* shows you things you really long for. There are all those graspable values floating around in the film. It's full of a lost heritage that we can't live. Life is no longer like that."

As I look back at the film's chaotic genesis, I share some of their mysticism and nostalgia. I like to think it achieved its final identity by some affinity with each successive generation of its youthful fans, until now, some thirty years later, no matter who made it or owns it in a legal sense, *Casablanca* belongs to its devotees of all ages.

WRITERS' ROOST

At Warners during the late thirties and early forties there was a convivial and cooperative spirit alien to movie production today, when filmmakers work in independent, separate units. Writers came and went, of course, but most were there on long-term contracts. About twenty-five of us occupied adjoining offices in the writers' building, including such well-known literary names as William Faulkner, James Hilton, Dalton Trumbo, John Howard Lawson, Ellis St. Joseph, Dudley Nichols, Christopher Isherwood, and, in other studios, George Kaufman, Moss Hart, Robert Sherwood, William Inge, Dorothy Parker, Robert Benchley, Aldous Huxley, James Agee, Preston Sturges, Herman and Joseph Mankiewicz, Bertolt Brecht, Garson Kanin, Lillian Hellman, and, for a time until his death, F. Scott Fitzgerald. With all its faults and foibles, it was Hollywood's most flourishing and fertile period in its concentration of talent, its social consciousness, and its dissemination of ideas, much as Greenwich Village had served twenty years earlier.

Some of the writers who had been more successful in other fields were apologetic about working in Hollywood, often proclaiming their misused talents all the way to the cashier. Granted, there was much that serious writers had to contend with: a mass production system with a tendency to "play down" to a supposed audience mentality, and submission to various censorship bodies. Most writers I knew did what they could to circumvent the system's limitations and often succeeded. When Warners turned out a film of merit and significance, there was a general satisfaction throughout the studio. If one of us was having trouble solving a story problem, it was common for another writer to offer suggestions even though no personal credit was involved. This was also true of some actors, producers, and directors.

Nor was studio life all serious. The writers' table, while perhaps not quite comparable in ambience to the Algonquin Round Table, was the scene of some lively banter and conversation. Practical jokes were frequent and inventive. One of mine worked almost too well.

It was April Fools' Day and John Huston was to be my target. For a year he had kept after Hal Wallis, Warners' production head, for a chance to direct a film. Today writer-directors are common, but at that time studios were more rigid in keeping their personnel in categories. A writer was there to write, a director to direct, and there was little crossing over. Finally, John was able to extract a promise that he could write and direct his next picture. By this time he had finished the screenplay, which he let me read. It was an excellent script with most of the business and even the camera angles carefully worked out, an almost predirected screenplay.

With my forgery project in mind, I went to the section of the story department where unproduced plays are filed. Letting her in on my plan, I asked the woman in charge to find me what she considered the most hopeless script among the huge pile of rejects. She came up with a long story treatment called *In Darkest Africa.* I had to read only a few pages to know this was one of the all-time lows in writing for the screen. I wrote an interoffice memo to Huston.

"Dear John: I know we promised to let you direct your next picture and intend to hold to our commitment. But first we want you to do the screenplay on the accompanying material which needs some rethinking, but we feel can make an important picture." And so help me, I signed Hal Wallis's name and sent the treatment to John with the memo attached.

Nothing happened for twenty-four hours and I began to wonder if the trick had misfired. It hadn't. In fact, it came dangerously close to getting John, if not fired, at least in trouble with the Warner front office. He came bursting into my room, evidently having traced the culprit through the story department. To my relief, John was laughing so hard he could scarcely tell me what happened.

"So *you* did it, you bastard."

I pretended innocence. "Did what? What are you talking about?"

"You know damn well what I'm talking about. That God-awful script."

I tried another tack. "Oh, you didn't like *In Darkest Africa?*"

"Like it? I was so fascinated I read every goddamn page right to the end."

I was laughing now, too. "John, for any sin you've ever committed, you've now done penance."

"You don't know the half of it. I was furious. All ready to direct my own picture, then that piece of shit thrown at me. I stormed Wallis's office. No appointment. Didn't even wait for the secretary to announce me. Just broke in and called Wallis every name I could think of. And I thought of some you couldn't put in print. Hal just sat there, his mouth open, without a clue to what it was all about. After I'd exhausted my vocabulary, he said, 'John, I never sent that script.' Then it dawned on him and he broke into a wide grin. 'It's April Fools'.'"

Among the studio executives, with some notable exceptions like Sam Goldwyn, there was a certain ambivalence in respect to writers. They were regarded as a special breed, separate but unequal, necessary but troublesome, independent and often irreverent toward studio authority. Also, it was in the nature of their work to have ideas and not always story ideas: in this period of a populist surge, their ideas were frequently considered radical, a potential threat to any corporate structure committed to the status quo. If scripts could have been turned out by a machine, I think most studio heads would have preferred it as a more tractable alternative.

This attitude was reflected in class distinctions among the studio personnel which extended even to the dining arrangements. Producers and directors, closer to the management, were welcome in the executive dining room where the lunches were of gourmet quality, but writers were invited only if they had just won an Academy Award. This happened to me after *Casablanca* and I can't say it was a privilege I wanted to repeat too often. The honored writer was seated next to Jack Warner at the head of the table where he was expected to laugh at the boss's constant stream of wisecracks.

So we had our own table in the main dining room where the food was less sumptuous but the atmosphere more relaxed. The third-class lunch was served cafeteria-style for the grips and technicians. So much for studio democracy.

Off the walk leading to the writers' building was a well-kept tennis court. In New York there had been neither the time nor the place for my favorite game. Now it was available at my doorstep. But when I tried to find someone to play with, I was warned that Jack Warner kept track from his office window of anyone using the court during working hours, which meant all day. I feel certain that was the most unused court in Hollywood, where tennis was popular on the estates of the more affluent movie people. But at Warners it was merely part of the scenery.

During the early forties, the war years, the movie industry took its turn making films on social themes, such as *Zola, The Grapes of Wrath, Casablanca,* and *I Am a Fugitive from a Chain Gang.* Since Warners was leading this trend, it was natural that many of its writers were politically conscious. To one degree or another they were involved in the struggle against fascism, in whatever form it appeared, and in working for a more democratic society, economically and racially. Today the label applied to us would be *left-wing,* but all labels are suspect; the word we used at the time to define our political activities and organizations was *progressive,* regardless of differing party affiliations or lack of them.

In our studio two of the leading activists in social-political causes were Dalton Trumbo and John Howard Lawson. Dalton was brilliant, witty, iconoclastic, Lawson more impassioned in his dedication. I remember that on my first day at the studio Jack Lawson made a visit to my office to welcome me with a handshake and a warm smile. Lawson believed in people and in their capacity to change their society for the better. If politics had been a religion, he would have made sainthood.

At the opposite political pole was Ayn Rand, employed for a brief time by the studio to write the screenplay based on her popular novel *The Fountainhead.* As I learned later, her family had been prosperous in Czarist Russia and had lost their fortune in the revolution. Whether or not this was the reason, Miss Rand had become fanatical on the subject of communism, socialism, or any "ism" except capitalism, which her books glorified. In fact, any movement of social concern, including the New Deal, was anathema to her. In later years she founded the cult which she calls objectivism—whose cornerstone is unbridled individualism, the God-given right of a power elite to impose its will on a less advantaged majority. Over the years she had gained a considerable following among people of her persuasion to whom she lectures and for whom she writes.

Needless to say, she did not have much of a following at Warners and kept herself pretty much isolated. My contact with her was a curious one. When Robert Rossen left Warners for Columbia Pictures, his office opposite mine was assigned to Miss Rand. Between our rooms was the outer office occupied by our secretaries. Her secretary passed the word to mine that Miss Rand wished not to be disturbed. Taking the hint, I made no effort to welcome her, which would have been natural in regard to a newcomer to the studio. At times when my door was open I caught her peeking in at me from her office as though I were some sort of alien creature she was studying from a discreet distance.

One winter day her scrupulous privacy broke down. It was pouring rain, and when it rains in California, which is seldom, the heavens open up and the gutterless streets are quickly flooded. Apparently Miss Rand had no car and at the end of this particular day was unable to get a taxi. Her secretary whispered to my secretary, asking whether I would let her ride with me as far as Hollywood on my way to the Elysée, where I was still living. So I crossed the forbidden threshold and said that, of course, I would be glad to take her. This was my first close look at her. She was small, dark-haired, thin-faced, with watchful eyes.

In the car I started a casual conversation and she responded, at first briefly then more volubly, as we drove down Cahuenga Pass to Hollywood Boulevard, her destination. I stopped the car. Before she moved, she looked straight at me.

"I didn't know you were this way at all."

I was surprised. "What way? What do you mean?"

She didn't answer until she had climbed out of the car and faced me. Her tone was as accusing as though I had committed eight of the seven deadly sins.

"You wrote *Mission to Moscow*."

Before I could make any response, she closed the door and hurried away.

I don't know what sort of person Miss Rand expected to find seated beside her, possibly a commissar in the guise of a screenwriter. At any rate, from that time on, although she kept her reserve, she was somewhat more friendly. But we never discussed either the film or politics.

Extracurricular politics was only one aspect of our lives during that period. Musso Frank's Restaurant on Hollywood Boulevard became the informal social club for screenwriters during the cocktail and dinner hours. The restaurant served excellent food, its menu consistent to this day. Without prearrangement, many of us gathered at tables of four or six in the rear of the wood-paneled taproom. Dry martinis, doubled without asking, washed away whatever problems we brought with us. Conversation flowed easily—the films we were working on, the front office foibles—and, of course, sex reared its beguiling head. Dates were often made or kept among the singles in the group, male and female. There were occasions when a divorced or separated wife ran into her ex-husband, but no blood was ever shed. They simply sat at separate tables.

William Faulkner was one of the habitués at Musso's and we met through a mutual friend, Tom Job, who had come to Warners after a comedy success on Broadway. Tom was easygoing, amusing, gregarious, the ideal companion for the introverted Faulkner. It was difficult to know Faulkner on any intimate terms. He was silent, reserved—at least until he had downed three or four martinis. I found him shy with the opposite sex. One evening I had an attractive partner at dinner and he was careful to keep Tom as a sort of buffer between himself and the young lady.

The famous story of Faulkner's Hollywood years centered on his request to "work at home," a privilege denied most writers under contract. Because of his literary prestige, the front office granted his request. Afterward he disappeared, no pages of his script were forthcoming, and no one could find him at the place where he had been staying. Finally he was traced to Oxford, Mississippi, which is what Faulkner meant by home.

Although screenwriters had much in common, there were wide differences both in ability and in attitudes toward their work. Some never aspired beyond the formula treatment of run-of-the-mill pictures, both A and B. They knew their craft and enjoyed the comfortable life it afforded, taking no risks with more demanding or controversial material. One of these was a roly-poly charmer, keen-witted and amiable, but a writer in name only.

Jerry Wald had acquired an almost legendary status by virtue of a story that circulated around the tables at Musso's. It seems that years earlier he had managed to corral two bright young college graduates, the Epstein twins, later to become my brief collaborators on *Casablanca*. They were born storytellers with wit and style. When they came to Hollywood they had neither money nor reputation. Jerry stowed them away in a modest Hollywood apartment where he brought them movie ideas, mostly garnered from newspapers or other periodicals, which they constructed into screenplays. He paid them each twenty-five dollars a week, barely enough to live on at that time, while Jerry's salary at Warners skyrocketed to the thousand-a-week range, mostly on the strength of their borrowed efforts. Jerry didn't tell the Epsteins that their stories were being produced, nor did he invite them onto the lot. He just gave them enough encouragement and salary raises to keep them slaving away on his behalf.

Then one day Jerry's bubble burst. The Epsteins went to a neighborhood theatre and, lo and behold, there on the screen was one of their stories just as they had written it. Indignant, they stormed the Warners gates and revealed how their talents had been misused and misappropriated. They were taken on as writers at a proper salary and given their proper credits.

And what happened to Jerry? Was he fired? Was he even reprimanded? On the contrary, he was promoted to the status of producer, in fact eventually one of the leading producers in the industry. By Hollywood reasoning, his coup with the Epsteins demonstrated that in a world that exists to create illusions, he was a master illusionist.

On the other end of the literary spectrum was a writer I had known in the Federal Theatre days. Born Ellis Joseph and brought up by an adoring mother in New York's then unfashionable East Side, he won a scholarship to the College of the City of New York, where he worked a transformation that was no less than a work of art. In a literal sense Ellis became a self-made man. He developed an accent that had nothing to do with his family origins. It is best described as mid-Atlantic, English enough to lend distinction, American enough to avoid the charge of snobbism. Then he sainted himself, becoming Ellis St. Joseph, a name in keeping with his brilliant literary talents.

In his late teens and early twenties he sold stories to such prestigious publications as *Harper's* and *Story Magazine,* some of them collected in anthologies. To supplement his income he gave lectures on Bernard Shaw at New York University. Few Americans could compare with Ellis in Shavian scholarship. He also wrote a clever comedy, *Three Ways to Rob a Lady,* which was performed by Federal Theatre units around the country. Agents courted him and lured him to Hollywood, where we renewed our friendship, which has lasted over the intervening years.

Before my arrival there, he had gained several screenplay credits but only one of them was made into a film of a quality worthy of his talents. It was a picture directed by Douglas Sirk, who remarked in a recent interview in *Film Comment,* ". . . the most brilliant dialogue I worked with was the script that Ellis St. Joseph did for *A Scandal in Paris.*"

Most directors and producers were both intrigued by Ellis's work and distrustful of its public acceptance. His writing was too original in style and concept to be pigeonholed into any of the familiar categories. In their estimation his scripts were highbrow for the tastes of the mass audience, so they were usually diluted by revisions and, in the process, lost the very quality that attracted them in the first place.

While in its social phase Warners was doing an antifascist film set in Poland during the Mannerheim, pro-Nazi regime before the war broke out. Vincent Sherman was to direct, Ida Lupino to star. At the time Ellis was out of work and I urgently recommended him for the screenplay. Ellis was given the assignment at a salary in keeping with the importance of the project. At the beginning Vincent and Ida were dazzled by the polished dialogue and elliptical style which flowed through the initial pages Ellis was submitting. The threesome became very intimate. Ellis was a new experience which they obviously enjoyed.

Suddenly, for some reason, the intimacy dissolved and with it their faith in the commercial prospects of Ellis's work. Since I had recommended him, Vincent came to me with an ultimatum. Ellis would be dropped from the picture unless I agreed to collaborate on the screenplay. To protect Ellis's credit, I accepted. My role was more that of peacemaker and insurer than writer. My "money credits," the kind that count in Hollywood, gave them the assurance they needed and most of the values in Ellis's script were preserved. Whatever I did in actual writing I was careful to keep in the style he had set. Vincent directed the film, *In Our Time,* with fidelity and dramatic flair, and Ida gave a strong and sensitive performance. The picture that eventuated was successful commercially and satisfying to us who had worked on it.

Since then, unfortunately, Ellis has been living more on his social graces than on his literary achievements, possibly the most undervalued writer in Hollywood's history. As the result either of the industry's lack of appreciation or of his own personal problems, he developed what is known as a "writer's block." He talked out his stories, mostly to friends on long telephone calls, pouring his literary gems into the black hole of the mouthpiece. On a visit to us in Palm Springs, he read us the first draft of an original screenplay whose theme was the last days of Hollywood epitomized in the tragic fate of an aging movie star. It seemed to us a superb script both in style and in the devastating irony of its content. In following years when I asked Ellis what he was doing, he was still rewriting the same screenplay. Recently, however, the much-revised screenplay has attracted a female star and a prospective producer. Better still, I found Ellis hard at work with a collaborator. Writing, not just talking. Perhaps the latter-day Saint has finally coalesced with the early Joseph and broken through the block. If so and if the circumstances are propitious, we can expect a film, original in style and meaningful in content.

Looking back from this perspective, how does a writer sum up his impressions of the "golden age" in Hollywood? In spite of the dross, its remembered virtues seem to outshine its sins. Today money, barefaced, sits in the producer's chair. Unless a picture is "big" in its cost and expected profits, it is too small to be visible. For subject matter there appears to be a preoccupation with decay and death—slow death, violent death, physical death, metaphysical death. Not only our films but contemporary plays and books all share this obsession.

I confess that this trend is disturbing. Are we being given these small injections of death to prepare us psychologically for its acceptance on some massive scale? I trust not. In the Hollywood period of which I am writing the mood was quite different. Death was regarded as a natural but unwelcome intruder into the living world, not as an end in itself. In myriad ways and in varying degrees of quality, our films celebrated life.

MISSION TO MOSCOW

Mission
Improbable

FADE IN

When I pencil in these two words on a blank sheet of paper, I have the same feeling as when I'm on a plane about to take off and I hear the exit door latch shut. I try not to think of metal (or mental) fatigue, of chance winds and sudden storms. Soon I will be thirty thousand feet above the earth with nothing to keep me there but a law of aerodynamics too complicated for me to understand. I commit myself on faith.

Even after writing some fifteen screenplays, I never start the next without the gnawing doubt of my ability to cope with the particular material. The imagination is a fragile craft for an uncharted flight to an uncertain destination. Once committed, I know I will have to live with my characters, sharing their conflicts and emotions. For four to six months, my outside life will be marginal, having less reality than the two-hour world I'm struggling to create.

A hundred or so pages later, assuming I've survived the journey, there will emerge a first-draft screenplay. It will have flaws but, I hope, it will establish the basic characterizations, mood, and story line. Film being a collaborative art (auteur theory to the contrary), my words will then have to filter through many hands and minds. Ultimately there will be a transition of creative authority to the director, who will become the dominant figure in the actual production.

This is perhaps the most crucial and controversial point in picture making. Assuming the writer and director are not the same person, the film's unity will depend on their reaching a shared point of view on the basic values to appear on the screen. A good movie will seem to have been made by one person when actually it will be a felicitous fusion of the work of many contributors, including the cinematographer, set designer, music composer, editor, and, of course, the actors who must bring it all to life. In the course of shooting, the director may add or subtract from what has been preconceived and committed to paper. In this respect I feel I have been more fortunate than many screen-writers, having worked with directors of the caliber of Ophuls, Wyler, Welles, Huston, Hawks, and Curtiz. More has been added to my scripts than subtracted.

From the start I had made a practice of turning down assignments whose subject matter was alien or of no interest to me. Since the accumulation of credits is the screenwriter's stock-in-trade, this involved a certain risk, including at times the displeasure of the front office, since contract writers were expected to accept whatever was assigned them. In the long run it worked to my advantage. I escaped the trap of being typed for one or another kind of movie whose repetition invited formula treatment. My credits, while fewer in number, ranged over a wide area, from action stories to those with more serious psychological and social themes. However, one assignment was not of my choosing. Looking back at its bizarre history, it seems incredible that the film was ever produced or even contemplated. In addition to the usual problems and hazards, it was the first of its kind to be made in a Hollywood studio and, up to now, the most controversial.

Having written the screenplays for a half-dozen pictures with scarcely a break, I'd been promised a leave of absence and was cleaning out my desk in the writers' building when the telephone rang. My secretary buzzed. "It's Mr. MacEwen. He wants to see you."

Walter told me Warners had bought a book, an important book they were eager to film. There was trouble, the chronic trouble; they had a script they couldn't use, a cast waiting in the wings, and an early shooting date. Would I postpone my vacation long enough to write the screenplay for *Mission to Moscow?*

From the newspaper reviews I was vaguely aware that the book, written by Joseph E. Davies, former ambassador to the Soviet Union, was a sympathetic account of his observations and experiences during the prewar years when he and his family were in Russia. Even though this was a period when the studios were making movies on social themes, a pro-Soviet semidocumentary seemed an unlikely choice for the Warner brothers, to whom capitalism was an article of faith. For my part, I was interested in sociological problems but, up to then, not in politics as such. I admired Franklin Roosevelt because I was conscious of a healthy change from the boom-or-bust, grab-what-you-can twenties to the more cooperative and humanistic era of the New Deal. But my knowledge of what was taking place inside the Soviet Union was scanty and unreliable. Ever since the Russian revolution the American news media were almost without exception anti-Soviet, so their reporting could hardly be considered objective.

Under these circumstances I felt that someone with more information on Soviet affairs would be better qualified to write the screenplay. But there were other reasons for my refusal. I had an ailing father back East whom I wanted to visit. Besides, I was too tired to do any assignment justice, let alone one involving special problems because of its controversial nature. Walter understood my reasons and I left the studio that night with a heady sense of freedom.

This came at the end of my third year in Hollywood. In all material ways the studio had treated me well. Starting as a very junior writer, I was now getting many of the choice assignments and my salary had been raised at nearly every option period. Money came easily and went easily as my increasingly extravagant habits kept pace with my income. I was still living in the Elysée, virtually in a garden, since sycamore trees and flowering bushes screened out the surrounding city. At night the velvet scent of jasmine drifted in through the tall French windows. I was reminded of Circe in the Odysseus legend, whose seductive gifts to their senses made the sailors forget their homes. I had not only forgotten home; I was no longer certain where it was.

Gradually I had become aware that another serpent inhabited Eden and this serpent was time. It slithered away, unnoticed. Only the calendars kept track of its passing, but who looks at calendars when one day is like the next and one month like another? Los Angeles had moods but no defined seasons. Depending on whether the wind blew from the desert or the sea, the air was dry or misty. In a seasonless world there are few punctuation marks. You knew when it was Christmas because Hollywood Boulevard became even more garish than usual with its colored lights and plastic Santa Clauses. People drank a good deal—more, I suspect, to forget than to celebrate the holiday.

In screenplays when we wanted to denote the passage of time, we used what was called a dissolve, indicating the closing and reopening of the camera's eye. This device enabled us to signal to the audience the passage of any period of fictional time necessary to the movement of the story. And so it began to seem with my life, pleasant as it was, that large portions were dissolving through an invisible gap. Change is our only way of measuring time and I realized that a change was necessary and past due. How it came about was beyond my expectations.

The next morning I was in my apartment packing for the trip when the phone rang. I had a premonition. *Don't answer.* The ringing outlasted my resistance. It was Mr. Warner's secretary. Come to his office immediately. A command from Olympus. When she said it was Mr. Harry Warner who wanted to see me, I was baffled. As president of the company, he ran its financial affairs but had little contact with its artists, least of all with writers who were far down on the studio totem pole.

Up to now I had seen the two Warners only at a safe distance. Jack, resplendent in a colonel's uniform of the U.S. Army (his military duties somewhat nebulous), was more in evidence. He could often be seen from my office window on his way to the executive dining room followed by a small entourage of assistants, secretaries, and agents. His jaunty stride suggested a bantam cock asserting his authority over the roost. Neither of the Warners had much to do with the actual production of their films except in matters of policy, which included a veto power over subject matter and star casting.

I was ushered into an imposing office large enough to accommodate a princely court. Seated at his desk was Harry Warner and standing at his shoulder, his brother, Jack. Both Warners—my God, what had I done? *Casablanca*, still not released, couldn't be *that* bad.

Their cordial greeting reassured me. Harry Warner began by thanking me effusively for my part of the work on *Casablanca* (Had it really turned out that well?), which he had just seen in the projection room. The elder Warner was a soft-spoken, grandfatherly man in his sixties, his rather ponderous manner in contrast to his off-the-cuff, wisecracking brother. He delivered speeches rather than talked to you, making conversation somewhat difficult. His rambling discourse was larded with personal reminiscences that were not always relevant to the subject at hand. Jack, not a patient type, was in the habit of interrupting,

although Harry never relinquished center stage without a struggle. The fraternal relationship suffered an uneasy balance of
power, with one brother occupying the throne and the other
being an ambitious pretender.

After a lengthy preamble Jack finally got sole possession of the
floor. He asked me why I had turned down the assignment just
offered me, his tone implying that evidently I didn't realize its
importance. I repeated the reasons I had given MacEwen.

With a nod Harry Warner deferred to his brother.

"Look, Koch, you can't turn this down."

I was surprised by his vehemence. Up to now they had permitted my rejection of unwanted assignments because the films
whose screenplays I had worked on had made the studio a
great deal of money.

Jack Warner took a turn at irony. "You've heard there's a
war on."

I smiled. "Yes, I've heard."

"Well, Russia's our ally," he said, and then as an afterthought,
"whether we like it or not."

Harry Warner was getting impatient. "Koch, what we're trying to tell you is this isn't just a studio matter. We're doing the
picture because our government wants it done."

"Our government?"

Mr. Warner allowed a pause to emphasize the importance of
his revelation. "The president of the United States . . . go ahead,
Jack, tell him."

Jack was more than willing. "I was invited to dinner at the
White House. Ambassador Davies was there—the fellow who
wrote the book. The president had it on the table beside him. He
handed it to me. 'Jack, I see you're in the army.' I had on my
uniform. 'As one officer to another, I suggest you do a film based
on this book. Our people know almost nothing about the Soviet
Union and the Russian people. What they do know is largely
prejudiced and inaccurate. If we're going to fight the war together, we need a more sympathetic understanding.' Or words to

that effect. Then Mr. Davies, who knew about it ahead of time, offered to work with the screenwriter in an advisory capacity." Ever the businessman, he added, "At no salary."

Flattered by the request, Jack Warner committed the studio on the spot without knowing the contents of the book. Nor, so it appeared, had he read it since. This was not unusual. Movie executives rarely read a book or screenplay, relying on an assistant to communicate the narrative in capsule form.

Although by nature a pacifist, I realized that the defaults and misjudgments of various European governments had allowed a situation to develop in Germany which seemingly left no alternative but war. Now the Warners were putting their request on patriotic grounds. How could I refuse to work on a project which the president of the United States considered important to the war effort? The answer was obvious—I couldn't. I did insist on certain conditions. I would begin working on the screenplay in the East, where I could confer with Mr. Davies and visit my father. Since time was important, I would need a secretary to help me while traveling. In addition, I asked for the right to select my own technical adviser, someone with personal experience in the Soviet Union whose veracity and objectivity I could trust. In this way I could check against information from other sources. The Warners accepted the conditions and agreed to pay all expenses, my own and those of the people who would assist me.

Finding a qualified secretary free to leave on a moment's notice was a problem. Besides the usual shorthand and typing requirements, I needed someone with critical judgment capable of digesting a vast amount of research material. Anne Taylor, my friend and former secretary, had all the necessary qualifications. When I called to ask her if she could join me on the assignment, she said she was about to begin a screenplay at Paramount. "Besides," she added pointedly, "I'm married"—a fact I had conveniently forgotten.

The evening before departure, Kaisa and I went to the Mo-

cambo, then Hollywood's "in" nightclub. I don't know whether I
was celebrating or trying to forget. In the course of the evening
I was called to the phone. Anne Taylor, who knew my habits and
habitats, had tracked me down to tell me she had solved my secretarial problem. A friend of hers wanted to visit her family in the
East and was interested in the project. The girl had been a
writer on a radio program with some previous secretarial experience in a New York advertising agency. On Anne's recommendation I agreed, sight unseen, and arrangements were made to
meet me at Union Station the next day for the noon departure of
the Santa Fe Chief.

Before planes came into common use, the Chief was a sort of
traveling extension of the movie colony. Moviemakers are per-
petual transients, shuttling back and forth over continents and
oceans. In the forties the usual destinations were Los Angeles and
New York, and the club car on the Chief was a meeting place for
celebrities. To me the Chief became associated with change beyond its geographical connotations. The original westward trip
to California had ushered in a new writing career. This journey
east, when I was weighed down with an unwanted responsibility,
began a complete transformation of my personal life.

My friend Ellis St. Joseph drove Kaisa and me to the station,
where a man from Warners was waiting with the travel documents. On the platform Kaisa and I did our parting scene in true
Hollywood style. Although neither of us said so, I think we both
knew that this good-bye was the end of what should never have
begun. Standing at a discreet distance watching this parting was
a girl who looked to be in her early or middle twenties. Preoccu-
pied with my two friends, I was not aware of who she was until
the conductor called "all aboard" and she came up to me to identify herself as my new secretary. I handed over her compartment
ticket and asked her to meet me in the dining car in half an hour.

The train was pulling out of the yards when I made a horrify-
ing discovery. I had left my entire research material, a half-

dozen books on the Soviet Union, including *Mission to Moscow,* in the trunk of Ellis's car. Now I had nothing with me to draw on for material to begin work on the screenplay.

I had glanced through the Davies book without studying it in enough detail to select what would be useful to dramatize. Three and a half days, the length of the transcontinental trip, would be lost when every day was precious on my tight schedule, especially at this early stage when I had hoped to have some approach to the film worked out to discuss with Mr. Davies. It was one of those moments when the situation seemed too hopeless for any possible remedy. I recall staring into the compartment mirror, hypnotized by that wan face staring back, while waves of self-pity rolled over me. I indulged in extravagant fantasies. I had messed up my life; now I was about to lose the war.

An hour passed, perhaps longer, when it suddenly occurred to me that the girl I'd seen briefly on the platform, my secretary-to-be, was waiting for me. It took a major effort to get to my feet and propel myself down the swaying aisles to the dining car. She was seated at a table reading a book. As I slid into the opposite seat, I looked at her closely for the first time. Unless I was too foggy to judge, she was pretty. Brown eyes, brown hair, brown traveling suit—all of a piece. Which was beside the point but not entirely. When I told her of the research material left behind, she didn't seem properly distressed.

"I guess you don't realize how serious it is."

"Well, we have one book with us." She held up the book she'd been reading—*Mission to Moscow.*

I was astonished. "Where did you get that?"

Instead of saying "at a bookstore," which was obvious, she anticipated my next question. "I thought I should know something about what you're doing."

For a moment I saw a glimmer of light on the distant horizon.

She rose. "While you're having your lunch, I'll see about the other books."

She was gone before I could ask her what she could possibly

do when our speeding train was separating us from those books
a mile a minute.

When she returned, she gave no explanation of what she'd
done and I didn't ask. I didn't want to know. I wanted to believe
in magic.

She had brought her stenographic pad back with her. "Where
should we work?"

"Work?" the idea took me unawares. I had set aside the afternoon for brooding. Anyway, I was too tired to work. I tried to
divert her. "You know, I'm so damn hazy today I've even forgotten your name."

"It's easy to forget. It's Anne Green." Was there a trace of
irony? I couldn't tell. She touched everything so lightly.

We worked.

We worked all afternoon. It began as a conversation. I asked
her what impressed her most about the book. She thought for a
moment. "I guess it's that a man as rich as Davies could see so
much that was good in a socialist country."

The remark suggested an angle. Play up the fact that our protagonist, a corporation lawyer married to the Hutton heiress,
reputed to be the world's wealthiest woman, had impressive
capitalist credentials. A vestige of my early legal training drifted
back from the distant past. The very best evidence in a court of
law is a statement against interest. By stressing Mr. Davies's conservative background, we might disarm some who would otherwise be skeptical of any report favorable to the Soviet Union.

With this in mind my first impulse was to begin the screenplay
with an illustrative sequence of the Davieses' affluent home life
before they left for Russia. On second thought I realized that it
was too bland an opening to catch the audience's interest. One
of the recurring problems was how to inform people without
boring them. Facts had to be presented in the guise of entertainment.

It was midafternoon before I could bring myself to dictate
those two words, *fade in*, which was like plunging into a lake

without knowing how to swim. As I cast around trying to piece together bits of a possible continuity, I discovered that my companion had oblique ways of expressing her reactions. When something in my rambling, trial-and-error dictation struck her as wrong, her pencil stopped. After a while I got the signal and reexamined the idea. Usually the pencil was right.

"That's an educated pencil you've got there. I'll try again."

In this hit-and-miss fashion we made some progress, but there was still no satisfactory opening sequence. By five o'clock I suggested we call it a day and go to the club car for a drink. She didn't move. "Couldn't we work until six?"

That frosty martini I'd promised myself receded into the future and I was a little disgruntled. Was this girl a Warner spy? Or perhaps an itinerant psychologist, since she had a way of drawing out my freely associated ideas, good or bad, while her pencil appraised their validity? In petty revenge I decided to stop talking to see how long she could endure complete silence. She outlasted me, and grudgingly, I went back to work.

And so it happened that between five and six that evening, as we passed through Needles on the California border, the opening sequence to *Mission to Moscow* emerged full-blown. I suddenly remembered having read Haile Selassie's moving speech before the assembly of the League of Nations in 1936 pleading for assistance against Mussolini's invading forces. Litvinov, the Soviet foreign minister (and friend of Davies's), had stood up in the assembly to pledge Russian military aid if the other Western powers would honor similar commitments to defend a fellow member of the League attacked by an aggressor. But the European allies hedged and vacillated; Litvinov's was the lone voice of the great powers raised in support of collective security against fascist aggression. Let the Soviet haters scream. This was fact, this was history.

If I've made all this sound unduly momentous, I am telling it the way it seemed at the time, under pressure and on notice that more was riding on this project than the success or failure of a movie.

The martinis came, two by two, against a background of the reddening Arizona desert framed in the club car windows. I found that Anne liked martinis and that we had grown up in nearby Hudson Valley towns. She used to swim in the same river I had fished for bass and perch some years earlier. By the second martini this seemed like quite a bond. By the third she confessed attending the opening night of a play of mine and had joined in with curtain calls for the author. Since the author was three thousand miles away, I was a little late in responding, but I decided she had excellent taste in drama. By this time my weariness had mysteriously vanished.

I was curious. "How did you get interested in politics?"

She thought for a moment. "Nearly everybody at Young and Rubicam, where I was working, was against Roosevelt."

"Except you?"

"And my boss. We were . . . well, like a couple of dogs in Venice. It's full of cats. In this case, fat cats."

"You didn't like advertising?"

She shook her head. "Nor any big business. I guess you could call me a socialist."

"I didn't call you anything."

She nodded. "Labels—they don't mean much, do they? Anyway I like *Mission*. . . . Shouldn't we work some more later?"

"Later? Oh, God, no. . . . Don't you ever let up?"

"In my high school graduation class book, do you know what they wrote under my picture?"

I put my guess in quotes. " 'This girl is bound to succeed and end the capitalist system.' "

She laughed. " 'The laziest girl in school.' "

The next morning I discovered Anne also had a sense of economy and a refreshing absence of inhibitions. I had just finished breakfast when she appeared and took the seat across from me.

The waiter came with the menu but she politely waved it aside and proceeded to eat the remains of my breakfast, some rolls and coffee in a pot. Not knowing we were together, the waiter was nonplussed but, trained in Pullman etiquette, he made no comment, and Anne calmly finished off her secondhand breakfast.

By the time the Chief arrived at Albuquerque, New Mexico, I had dictated fifteen pages of first-draft screenplay, leaving space for Selassie's speech, which Anne would research in New York.

By Trinidad, Colorado, I discovered that Anne's shorthand was a melange of Pitman symbols, words written out, and pictograms, decipherable only by her.

By Dodge City we had a second sequence—the Davies home (whatever and wherever it was) and their departure for Moscow roughly outlined.

By Kansas City, Missouri, I had conclusive evidence that Anne was a poor typist.

By Keokuk, Iowa, I found out that she couldn't spell.

By Springfield, Illinois, I knew it didn't matter. Stenography is available everywhere. Wit and wisdom are rare commodities, especially in someone so young.

As we stepped off the Chief in Chicago to change trains, the Santa Fe station master handed me the research books left behind in Los Angeles. By now nothing surprised me about Anne. She dealt in her own kind of magic.

By the time we reached New York, we had a rough treatment for the first half of the screenplay. From the nearly disastrous start, I now had enough to discuss with Mr. Davies.

Later, as the work progressed, I knew Anne was indispensable to the project—and to my life. I asked her if she would sign a long-term, exclusive contract (like mine with Warners).

She said, "With options?"

I agreed. "Every seven years."

That was thirty years ago. We've taken up all the options.

THE WRITER –

At age eight

Howard Koch at the "Writers' Roost"
at the Warner Building in Hollywood

Getting married, in
Yuma, Arizona (1944)

Wife Ann and son Peter
at home in Palm Springs

Max Ophuls and Howard Koch
during the preparation period
for *Letter from an Unknown
Woman* (1948) in Palm Springs

AND HIS WORK:

"INVASION FROM MARS"

Orson Welles reading
Howard Koch's script
for the notorious
broadcast of 1938
THE MUSEUM OF MODERN
ART/FILM STILLS ARCHIVE

THE SEA HAWK

Errol Flynn as Thorpo
in Warners' 1940 release

Gale Sondergaard
and Bette Davis
in Warners'
The Letter, 1940
THE MUSEUM OF
MODERN ART/ FILM
STILLS ARCHIVE

THE LETTER

SERGEANT YORK

Margaret Wycherly
and Gary Cooper in
Warners' 1941 movie

CASABLANCA

Two scenes from the
famous classic of 1942
starring Humphrey Bogart
and Ingrid Bergman

Dooley Wilson is at the piano

NO SAD SONGS FOR ME

Wendell Corey and Margaret Sullavan
toasting the New Year in Columbia's 1950 release

THE WAR LOVER

Steve McQueen,
Shirley Ann Field,
and Robert Wagner
on location

Sandy Dennis, Keir Dullea,
and Anne Heywood in a
scene from the 1968 movie
THE MUSEUM OF MODERN
ART/ FILM STILLS ARCHIVE

THE FOX

An Island
Kingdom

When I called Mr. Davies for an appointment, he invited me to
his camp on Lake St. Regis in the Adirondack Mountains. The
word *camp* puzzled me. Were they living in tents and cooking
over open fires? Not usual for people in their circumstances, but
then Mr. Davies, I assumed, was an unusual man or he wouldn't
have written *Mission to Moscow*.

At his suggestion I brought Hardy with me, my twelve-year-
old son, who was looking forward to roughing it more than I
was. When we got off the train at St. Regis station, the Davies
limousine was there to meet us. The chauffeur drove us to the
edge of a lake, where we transferred to a motor launch with a
crew of three men in yachtsman uniforms. When the captain
pointed out the "camp" perched high on an island cliff, Hardy
was taken aback. "That's not a camp, it's a town."

"Kingdom" would have been more accurate. An island kingdom, self-sufficient like a fief of feudal days. We were met at the wharf by the official guest greeter, who escorted us into a small elevator which carried us up the two-hundred-foot cliff. By now Hardy had forgotten about roughing it; he was intrigued and so was I.

Scattered over the island, each with complete privacy, were a dozen or so modern guest houses of cedar wood with colorful designs on the outside walls. They were later identified as dachas, Russian-style country houses. One of these was ours for the duration of our stay. Our escort showed us a panel of pushbuttons, each with the name of a service at our disposal—maid, valet, food, drinks, nurse, guide, or what-have-you. Instructing us to come to the Indian museum at six to meet our hosts, the guest greeter left us to our Alice-in-Wonderland musings. After a tour of our elegant quarters, Hardy gave his considered opinion: "Some camp."

The Indian museum was a long, rambling building modeled on the longhouses of the Iroquois nation, the confederation of Indian tribes that once inhabited the region. In the glass showcases was a large collection of Indian handicrafts. At one end of the museum, drinking cocktails, were Mr. and Mrs. Davies and a number of guests, including Robert Buckner, a writer-turned-producer, who had been selected by the studio to supervise the production.

Mr. Davies was a vigorous man in his fifties with graying hair and a warm smile. Although not quite as handsome as he would be portrayed by Walter Huston, he made an impressive appearance in the green and gold braided jacket he wore as Commodore of Lake St. Regis Yacht Club. Mrs. Davies, somewhat younger, was a beautiful woman with a kind of smooth, marble perfection of features and ease of manner often found in those born to wealth. (Perhaps Fitzgerald was right—the rich *are* different.) Her daughter, later to become Dina Merrill, the movie actress, was a pretty girl in her teens. They were gracious hosts, particularly attentive to Hardy, who wasn't old enough to draw on martinis for social sustenance.

From the museum we moved to the main house, where dinner was served in a baronial dining room with enormous windows on either end overlooking Lake St. Regis and the surrounding mountains. Mr. and Mrs. Davies sat at opposite ends of the long table with twenty or so guests in between. Sitting next to Mrs. Davies, I had an opportunity to get her view of the Soviet Union. She left politics to her husband but told me some revealing anecdotes. I made a mental note of one that might be useful to the film in illustrating American misconceptions of Russia as a primitive country. It seems the Davies family were very fond of ice cream. On their first trip to Moscow they took along gallons frozen in special containers. The Russians were amused. Living in a cold country, they had no trouble freezing their own ice cream.

Glancing around the handsome room with its affluent guests and liveried servants, I wished for a cameraman. No Warners set could do it justice. On the Chief we had tried to imagine the wealthy ambassador's home and family life, but this was far beyond our preconceptions. There could hardly have been a more incongruous setting for a man whose career was now tied to his espousal of an anticapitalist country.

That evening I took stock of what I considered the pluses and minuses of my various associates on the project. Bob Buckner, associate producer, was a conservative. He and his wife were models of southern respectability. By judicious investing (an art I never mastered) he had parlayed his large salary into a small fortune. I figured he would probably go along with *Mission* because of Davies and the Warners but not with enthusiasm for the subject matter.

Bob told me that Michael Curtiz had been selected to direct the film. As much as I appreciated Mike's talents in directing action pictures, I felt he was miscast for a film in which most of the action would be verbal exchanges. I had heard that in his younger days Mike had been involved in revolutionary politics in his native Hungary, but if so, he had left them there. In America he was strictly apolitical. And he was a worrier, accustomed to success and fearful of box-office failure.

Walter Huston was to play Ambassador Davies—a distinct plus. A fine actor, he exuded charm and goodwill. Given the right material, he would make his ambassadorial role credible and authentically American.

For the ambassador's wife, Ann Harding had been cast—another plus. An accomplished actress, she bore a striking resemblance to Mrs. Davies, physically and in the social poise that suggested similar backgrounds.

Eleanor Parker, who would play their daughter, was a recent addition to the Warners "stable." I knew nothing of her acting ability, but at least she would be a new face on the screen.

Oscar Homolka was a perfect choice for Litvinov. He was one of the best of the European actors who had come to this country. The other, smaller, roles would be as nearly as possible typecast in appearance and mannerisms. These included Roosevelt, Schacht, Stalin, Churchill, Molotov, and assorted Russians, Americans, and Germans.

And what about my role as the writer? At least until the script was finished, I would be dead center, trying to cope with all these diverse personalities, interests, and political attitudes. On the trip east I had gained confidence as scenes began to take shape. By the time we had reached New York, my mood was almost euphoric, abetted no doubt by Anne's companionship. Now my original doubts were returning and I was not at all certain that I was the right casting for the role. Could I write convincingly about a way of life of which I had no previous experience and about a controversial and somewhat mysterious country in which I had never set foot?

Lying in bed that night, I thought back to my mother's vicarious identification with the rich and famous who peopled settings such as this island kingdom. Is there some psychic connection? Do we unconsciously seek ways to fulfill whatever dreams are instilled in us at an impressionable age? Or is it all pure chance? . . . I glanced at Hardy asleep in the other bed. Was he dreaming about castles and kingdoms or, much more likely, about the next day's promised fishing on Lake St. Regis?

The next morning while the guide took Hardy out on the lake, the conference began in Mr. Davies's study. With some trepidation I waited for their reactions as he and Bob Buckner read copies of the proposed continuity Anne and I had worked out on the train. Buckner read it quickly and signaled his approval. Having been sent east by the Warners to check on progress, he was as anxious as I to mail back pages to Curtiz, whose acceptance was needed before they could be mimeographed and sent to the various departments that would be involved in the production.

Less accustomed to screen treatments, Mr. Davies took more time in reading. Up to now I had been so immersed in getting something down on paper that I had not fully realized the delicate problem in using part of a man's life as dramatic material with the person still alive and, in this instance, in the same room. Film biographies were usually made about people long since dead and in no position to raise objections.

To Bob's relief and mine, Mr. Davies's initial reaction was very warm. He liked opening on the scene in the League of Nations and most of the continuity as far as we had gone. However, I sensed he had some reservations over the liberties I had taken with the order and location of events. If an incident in the book had occurred in Leningrad at a certain time, I felt no compunction in moving the scene to Moscow at a later or earlier date in the interests of a more logical continuity.

Since life doesn't arrange events to suit the convenience of a dramatist, I felt I had to make a distinction between changing an inconsequential fact and distorting the essential attitudes and actions of the historical characters we were portraying. I wasn't certain Mr. Davies was entirely convinced, but at the time he accepted the distinction with good grace.

More difficult to deal with was his tendency to oververbalize instead of letting the images tell the story whenever possible. Like a good trial lawyer, he wanted to be certain that all the evidence got to the jury and was made so obvious that the most obtuse juror would be sure to get the point—a tactic more appropriate to the courtroom than to the theatre. Nor could we possibly encompass all the ideas, observations, and experiences he considered important during his ambassadorship. As tactfully as I could, I pointed out that such a picture would run much longer than the required two hours. A film or a play can never be a literal transcription of life. By a process of selection a dramatist extracts what is essential to evoke an imaginative response from the audience.

By this time I had learned that a screenwriter, to function effectively, must try to understand not only the psychology of his characters but that of his associates as well. He has to cope with criticism and suggestions coming from sources with the authority to pass on his work. This normally included director, producer, and sometimes the star. *Mission to Moscow*, I realized, would have additional complications. The studio heads, possibly the Warners themselves, would be fine combing the script to check on matters of policy. And Mr. Davies had been given the contractual right of screenplay approval. For obvious reasons, a studio rarely accorded an author this privilege when acquiring a literary property.

The ways of coping with script interference vary, of course, with the personalities involved. In any collective effort of a creative nature, individual egos must be considered and nourished, one's own as well as those of the other participants. If a useful suggestion comes from an authoritative source, I make a great deal of it. Appreciation makes the other person more amenable if later I reject some suggestion I consider damaging. If he insists, I have to decide whether it's worth making it an issue. Often I have found it prudent to compromise on a small point in order to gain a more important one. However, when some value basic to the integrity of the story or characters is at stake, a writer who cares about his work must be ready to resist in any way he can, even if it involves an unpleasant confrontation.

In my conferences with Mr. Davies I quickly realized I was dealing with a professional diplomat quite capable of seeing through my amateur ploys. I would have to make every effort to avoid a showdown on a script issue since he had more influence than I. Not that he would use it capriciously; he was too intelligent for that. He respected professionalism and listened carefully to an opposing point of view. In fact, our relationship at this time could hardly have been more harmonious. He went beyond the confines of the book in providing us with intimate details of the Soviet leaders, some useful to the film, and in correcting some of my misconceptions of the Soviet economic system.

By this time I felt free to clear up something that was much on my mind, relating to his role as the protagonist of our film.

"Mr. Davies, I'd like to ask you a very personal question."

"Go ahead."

"You're obviously a wealthy man, a capitalist. How do you reconcile this with your advocacy of a Communist country?"

"Let me correct something right at the start—and this is important to the film. The Soviet Union is not a Communist country. It has a Communist party which many Russians belong to, but its economy is socialist."

"How do you distinguish?"

"Every Russian I ever talked with said they had achieved a socialist state but they were still a long way from communism, which to them meant 'from each according to his ability and to each according to his need.' "

"If that's their ideal, what's stopping them?"

Mr. Davies pondered his answer. "Human nature. Man is competitive and I believe the capitalist system, the American system, with all its faults, preferable because it accords with reality and with individual liberty."

"Still you see merit in the Soviet system."

"Russia's our ally against fascism. That's more important than our differences. Anyway, I put in the book what I saw and heard while I was there. I tried not to be prejudiced and the film should do the same."

"I agree. At first I didn't want to do the screenplay but I've learned something and now I want to very much."

"I sensed that. And we'll get along."

When I left St. Regis, Mr. Davies turned over to me several volumes of transcripts of the controversial Moscow trials of 1938, including notes he had made during the proceedings. Some of these in condensed form were to find their way into the film and became the main targets of anti-Soviet attacks after the film was shown in this country.

Returning to New York, my first task was to find a qualified technical adviser. Again, as in the case of my more-than-secretary, I had a stroke of good fortune. Jay Leyda was a film critic–historian, self-educated, from a small Ohio town where he had been brought up very properly by two maiden aunts. Nothing in his background or in his well-scrubbed, boyish appearance suggested his unconventional and nomadic life-style. In his early twenties he had ventured to the Soviet Union, where he learned the language and eventually became an assistant to the Russian director Eisenstein, whose books he translated into English. In later years he established film libraries in various countries over the world and wrote a number of scholarly filmographies and biographies, including *The Melville Log*, which became the definitive source book for readers and students of that author.

At our first meeting I sensed that I had found a valuable ally.

While sympathetic to the Soviet system, he was scrupulously honest and not blind to its shortcomings. I came to regard him as the Sherlock Holmes of researchers. No fact was too elusive for him to track down. Reserved by nature, Jay had no small talk. Everything he said was stripped down to its essentials. Nouns and verbs predominated; adjectives were used very sparingly. With his fidelity to authentic details, he was to serve as a counterweight (and sometimes irritant) to Curtiz and various heads of the production department, many of whose ideas about the Soviet Union, its mores and customs, were hangovers from Czarist Russia.

While still in New York a telegram arrived from Bob Buckner, who had gone back to the studio: FIRST 22 PAGES OF SCRIPT EXCELLENT. CURTIZ JOINS ME IN CONGRATULATIONS. PLEASE SEND BACK AS MUCH MORE AS POSSIBLE. URGENTLY NEED IT FOR ALL DEPARTMENTS. BEST REGARDS.

While this was encouraging, past experience forewarned me that these reactions were not necessarily final.

Since the work seemed to be going well, I decided to stay in the East as long as the studio permitted, hoping to complete a first draft before the inevitable story conferences so dear to producers and so hazardous to writers. With Warners picking up the tab, I felt we, the "we" including Anne, should treat ourselves to the most ideal conditions for work and pleasure. We chose Lake Mohonk in the Shawangunk Mountains a hundred miles north of New York City, close enough to Kingston so that I could visit my father.

The Mohonk Mountain House is a unique American institution. For a hundred years it has been run by successive generations of the same Quaker family, the Smileys. As a recent concession to the twentieth century, the stringent rules that once barred automobiles and alcohol as twin evils have been relaxed. The nineteenth century still lingers in the spacious halls lined with photographs of its many celebrated guests—presidents, Supreme Court justices, famous authors and naturalists, representative figures in different periods of our history. Early conservationists, the Smileys had preserved their thirty-square-mile mountain domain (recently declared "forever wild") in its natural state.

Besides the mountain house itself, the only man-made additions are a network of forest trails and an occasional roughwood, Japanese-style summer house built at lookout points and blending into the surroundings. Standing high on a cliff, the rambling house overlooks the Esopus Valley and the Catskills (John Burroughs country) on one side and the emerald green waters of Mohonk Lake on the other. Of glacial origin, the lake is so deeply embedded in its granite cliffs that until recently it was reputed to be bottomless.

There is a current expression, somewhat exaggerated, that Mohonk is "for the newlyweds and the nearly deads." Anne and I didn't quite fit into either category, but we quickly adapted to a pleasurable routine of working in the morning and early afternoon, then taking long walks or horseback rides over the mountain trails. Hardy came with us as a chaperon of sorts, being well suited by virtue of age, twelve, and by temperament, discreet and affectionate.

Amused and touched, Anne told me that Hardy had drawn her aside and made an effort to find out whether she would work out as a possible stepmother.

"How long have you known Dad?"

"Not very long. Just on this trip."

"He must be sorta lonely—I mean stuck out there in Hollywood."

Anne sensed what Hardy wanted to know. "He misses you and Karyl. He told me that."

The boy's face lit up. "He said that?"

"Yes, and he meant it."

"We miss him too."

This conversation brought home to me that as a father I had left much to be desired. Perhaps things would change now. With help from Anne, I was learning more from *Mission* than about the Soviet Union.

We followed the Quaker rules faithfully except when they interfered with our natural inclinations. Since alcohol was taboo, we provided our own, drinking our homemade cocktails, and Hardy his Cokes, in an isolated summer house. The countryside, which stretched out far below us, was a pleasing backdrop to the private world we were creating in idyllic surroundings. Hollywood was three thousand miles away, a distance that our thoughts rarely traversed.

During one of my "thinking periods" Anne learned from a younger Smiley of an interesting event that took place on their mountaintop some forty years before. The background was The Hague Disarmament Conference that had been held in Holland at the turn of the century. It seems that our leaders, euphemistically labeled statesmen, change very little over the ages. The Hague conference ended the same way as our contemporary disarmament meetings between us and the Russians—by increasing armament instead of reducing it, thus making their citizens pay out tax money for the dubious privilege of being able to kill each other with more efficiency and multiplicity. The failure of The Hague conference actually instigated a rush by the various participating nations to build weapons at a faster rate in preparation for World War I.

Because the conference was a mockery of its high-sounding intentions, Andrew Carnegie conceived the idea of holding an American disarmament conference, the first in our history, to counteract the disillusioning results at The Hague. Many leaders in different fields, including former President Cleveland, President Lowell of Harvard, Mark Twain, and John Burroughs, were invited to take part. The place chosen for the peace conference was appropriate to the Quaker tradition of nonviolence—Mohonk Mountain House.

This historical event had little to do with *Mission to Moscow* but it seemed to fit in with our mood. By now Anne and I were emotionally involved with each other and with the project that had brought us together. Logic had nothing to do with it. We felt, or perhaps we could claim *sensed*, that the future of all of us hung in the balance of what happened between the two giants—the United States and the Soviet Union. If we could make even the slightest contribution to their understanding and acceptance of each other, it would be a source of satisfaction.

Neither of us could anticipate the coming Cold War, which began roughly with the death of Roosevelt and was later officially proclaimed by Churchill at Fulton, Missouri. At this point we were allies, each depending on the other, the Russians fighting off the Nazi invaders on a thousand-mile front while we furnished supplies and made ready the Channel crossing and the second front. The war had to be finished but the issue was already decided, and our concern was the kind of peace that would come out of it. By good fortune we were living and working in an atmosphere that nourished our hopes. Looking back, I see this as the idyllic phase of our *Mission to Moscow* experience. It is in the very nature of an idyll that it has to end.

The
Production

The studio was becoming restive and we couldn't stretch out our eastern interlude any longer. We arranged to make the return trip with Jay Leyda, who had spent the intervening time selecting stock footage from the Artkino Film Library—shots indicated by our script as far as we had gone. He was waiting for us on the train platform. Standing at his side was a slender girl in her twenties, small in stature but with a commanding presence, pleasing features, and flashing dark eyes. In her hand she carried a large, curved sword.

Jay introduced us to his wife, Si-Lan Chen, a leading Chinese–West Indian dancer whom he had met and married in Russia. The exotic Si-Lan was as outspoken as her husband was reticent. Her tongue could be sharper than her sword (a dance prop) but was never edged with malice. Her background was even more varied than Jay's. Her father was secretary to Sun Yat-sen, the first elected president of the Republic of China. He had married a Trinidadian and had taken his family to China. Growing up in the official circles and close to Madame Sun, Si-Lan had become acquainted with their military commander, Chiang Kai-shek, and thoroughly despised him even before he became a reactionary warlord. After Sun's death, Si-Lan's father, Eugene Chen, became foreign minister.

One memory typified her relationship with Chiang Kai-shek. On a family outing, Chiang challenged her to a race up a mountain. She was first at the top. Feeling disgraced by being bested by a girl, Chiang vented his temper on her and sulked for the remainder of the outing. When Chiang took over power, Madame Sun and the Chen family with Si-Lan fled the country and went to Russia, where her career as a dancer flourished.

In the first part of our cross-country trip together, Si-Lan was somewhat reserved and watchful. We felt we were being appraised, which was understandable on the part of someone new to the country thrown together with strangers on a project dealing with the Soviet Union, for which she had deep feelings. Once we were accepted, she spoke freely and later made her own contributions to the dance numbers selected for the film.

By the time we returned to Hollywood we had a scene outline for the entire picture and about half the screenplay. So far there had been no outside interference. Anne plowed through hundreds of pages of the Moscow trials testimony and other material, giving me the substance in digest form. After discussions with her and Jay I would write the scenes and often rewrite them following their appraisal before turning them over to Buckner and Curtiz. It was going too smoothly to last.

Pressures began to accumulate as soon as the shooting commenced. Interoffice memos started flying in all directions, a sure sign of mounting tensions. One from Jack Warner, more involved

with this project than was his custom, showed his concern:
"Please *step* on it!"

I replied:

I'm very pleased that you like the script. I can understand that
the pages seem to be coming to you rather slowly, but this picture presents so many problems of every kind that I revise scenes
three and four times before sending them through. My purpose is
to give you as nearly the final script the first time, as I possibly
can. The 104 pages which are now finished are the survivors of
four times that many which have gone into my wastebasket.

However, I promise you that I shall continue to keep the script
a safe distance ahead of the director during the home stretch of
the remaining third of the picture.

Sincerely,
Howard Koch

At the same time Jay, rushing back and forth between my
office and the set, was having his troubles keeping the reproduc-
tion of Soviet life as authentic as possible. With unconscious
humor Mike Curtiz gave him his first instructions. "Your job is
to make everything accurate, but don't forget I have to take liberties."

Others were "taking liberties" that distressed Jay, particularly
the music department. Jay appealed to Buckner for support.

To MR. ROBERT BUCKNER
From MR. JAY LEYDA

Instead of brooding over it, I think I should tell you about a
worry of mine: the problem of this film's music. The score has
been put in very capable hands [Steiner's] but the Russian expert
who has been assigned to him has already given me so much pain
on this film that I can't be very hopeful about his contribution at
this stage. Max Rabinovich has been the *de facto* technical ad-
visor on "Mission to Moscow"—at least on the set—because he
always told Mike what Mike wanted to hear, which is the part of
my job that I've been very slow in learning. If Rabinovich is
allowed to advise on the Russian themes for Steiner's score, I am
sure that all the band music will sound like a 1910 band concert

in the Odessa park and all the folk tunes will have the flavor of an emigré Russian vaudeville act. Rumors from the Music Department confirm my worst suspicions. This seems an unnecessary risk to take when there is so much excellent and genuine material available for each of music spots in the film.

Will you worry about this a little further? If you want me to go into detail, I'll be glad to.

J.L.

Jay's problems with authenticity were not only musical. They extended into every phase of Soviet life—their culture, architecture, dress, education, social customs, recreation, military procedures, even their flora and fauna, as the following illustrates:

Cutter (to Jay): "Now don't tell me there aren't any camels in the Ukraine. This is a great shot, I've got to use it."

There was a space in Kalinin's (president of the Soviet Union) office to be filled with something innocuous, so that no one could accuse Warners of gilding the lily. They decided on a map of the Soviet Union. They leafed through their numerous Russian books and found what they were looking for—the right size and color and everything—but there were no city names on it, so Jay was called over to scatter Russian names over it.

Jay, in a tense but quite controlled voice: "You've picked a map of the Moscow sewage system."

We can hope it was not an attempt at symbolism.

One day when I was on the set Mike Curtiz called down to me from his perch on the boom:

"Listen, Koch, we need a scene somewhere where Davies opens his protocol."

"His what?"

"His protocol—that black case he's always carrying around."

"You mean his portfolio. *Protocol* is a word for diplomatic formality."

"Never mind then—too goddamn much formality in this picture anyway."

A call from Harry Warner was a more serious matter. He and

his brother had been looking at the daily rushes and were having some second thoughts. Since visual action comes across much more compellingly than the same content on paper, they were beginning to have capitalistic qualms about portraying the Soviet Union in a favorable light. Couldn't we tone it down a bit or inject more sins into our characterizations of the Russian leaders? For instance, they probably traded favors, quid pro quo, with their corporations, lining their own pockets like many American politicians. Why now show that in a scene?

Drawing on what I had learned from the Davies book and from other sources, I explained that, whatever the Soviet sins, they were not the same as ours. In the first place, there *were* no private corporations. While there were disparities in income—a commissar or professional or an artist was paid more than a clerk or an unskilled laborer—it was not possible to amass great fortunes, either honestly or dishonestly, because the means of production were publicly owned and there was no area for private speculation and profit. Although Mr. Warner was not exactly happy with this explanation, he had no desire deliberately to pervert the facts. Besides, the production wheels were turning; it was too late to shift gears. In a sense the Warner brothers had trapped themselves into making a film with which they were not entirely in sympathy.

About midway through the shooting Ambassador and Mrs. Davies, along with their entourage, arrived at the studio. Everyone was a little nervous, wanting to make sure that the right things would be said to an author who was protected by an excellent contract. Harry Warner himself piloted the party down to the stage, where the prop man displayed properly named chairs for the distinguished visitors.

The trouble started on the first day. Mr. Davies looked over the actors, looking longest at Walter Huston, who was playing the ambassador. Finally, when Curtiz sidled up to him, Mr. Davies spoke his mind.

"There's one thing I can't understand. You've made an effort in casting and makeup to have all the other characters resemble the originals—Roosevelt, Kalinin, Churchill, Litvinov. But Mr. Huston doesn't look like me."

"But, Mr. Davies, all these other people are well-known men."

There was a horrified silence, except for a slight giggle from one of the crew.

"What do you mean?" Davies replied. "I'm well known. I have thousands of friends."

Curtiz had no answer, at least none that would appease Mr. Davies. In view of the film's overall purpose, this seemed like a minor objection that Mr. Davies would drop. Instead, he took his complaint to the front office. The Warners, who had some misgivings about the film's commercial prospects, insisted that Huston appear as his own attractive self, which would help sell the picture. For a few days, with no relenting on either side, there was talk of canceling the production even though the studio was heavily involved financially. Jay, Anne, and I shared the general suspense, since all our work would go down the drain, and by now our interest in having *Mission to Moscow* reach the American people was more than a professional concern. Since the question of an actor's makeup was not in a writer's province, I had so far stayed out of the argument.

Finally a compromise was worked out: Mr. Davies would be permitted to appear on the screen as himself at the opening of the picture. For this prologue he wrote his own speech. When I read it, I was dismayed. In essence it was a long, drawn-out statement to assure the audience that, in spite of the favorable things about the Soviet Union noted in his book and in the film, he was a true-blue capitalist who believed in free enterprise, the pioneer spirit, motherhood, and apple pie.

No one connected with the production, except Mr. Davies, liked the idea, and everyone hoped that I, as the writer responsible for the script, could prevail on him to change his mind. I pointed out that the film's content made his devotion to the capitalist system abundantly clear. There was no need for a verbal apologia which would precondition the audience and dilute the content of the film. Moreover, we would be asking viewers to accept Huston as Ambassador Davies, an illusion hard to sustain after they had already seen the real Mr. Davies. As I pressed my objections as strenuously as I could, I saw that it was a hopeless effort. I was gaining nothing but Mr. Davies's growing resentment. Up to now he had endorsed my script pretty much as I wrote it, but he was in no mood to listen to a writer's argument on a matter of policy already conceded by the Warners. I remember he angrily dismissed my objections by saying that I didn't understand the emotional effect of his proposed speech because I was too "paled over by sickly thought." I recognized the Shakespearean reference, but I decided that on this subject Mr. Davies didn't want "thought," sickly or otherwise. The scene was shot and shown during the early exhibition of the film, but I heard that later the speech was dropped.

It was difficult to understand Mr. Davies's insistence on this point when, in most other respects, his suggestions had been reasonable. Jack Warner made a shrewd guess that he had his eye on the presidency and that the film was, in a sense, his opening gun. Certainly he had many things working for him—his wealth and position, his effective ambassadorship in establishing good relations with a powerful ally, and, perhaps most important, his lifelong friendship with Franklin Roosevelt. What he still lacked was massive public exposure, and this the film could provide. Mr. Davies was an ambitious man and he may have had this in mind. However, it would be an oversimplification to assert that his only motive was personal. I'm convinced that he sincerely believed, as did Roosevelt, that future world peace hinged on the continuation of friendly relations between the United States and the Soviet Union and that *Mission to Moscow* would make an important contribution to a mutual understanding. With the death of Roosevelt and the advent of the Cold War this dream faded, and with it the political career of Ambassador Davies.

No matter how favorable the initial reactions to a screenplay, once concessions are made it becomes open season for criticism and demands for changes. I was having increasing difficulties with Mike Curtiz. He had little interest in the political content, one way or another. But the "talk scenes," as he called them, between Davies and Stalin and with other Soviet and Allied leaders worried him. In his previous pictures, conflicts were resolved with fists or guns. In our film, differing points of view and objectives had to be couched in terms appropriate to diplomatic usage. Mike felt more at home with the obvious dramatic elements—the roundup of the alleged conspirators and their trial and, of course, the battle scenes on the Russian front for which Jay was able to procure some remarkable newsreel shots of the German invasion and the Russian defense.

As it turned out, the "talk scenes"—which Mike, despite his reservations, shot very well—proved fascinating to audiences, both here and in Russia, no doubt for the reason that the general public are not privy to the private conversations of high-level officials on matters of international policy. Ambassador Davies had made copious notes immediately after conferring with Soviet and other Allied leaders, so that we were able to present the actual give-and-take exchanges, at least in condensed form.

Now came trouble from an unexpected source. Robert Buckner, occupied with production details, had been content to leave the script problems in my hands. Suddenly a batch of pages with a whole new ending came through to me from mimeograph. Without consulting me, he simply had exercised his prerogative as producer and his former status as writer. My ending had used a familiar biblical quotation which, in visual terms, emphasized the hope of peace instead of closing on the war itself. As the Russians had been forced to turn their plowshares into swords, they would then be able to turn their swords back into plowshares. Buckner's ending seemed to me conventional and repetitious. With Buckner's refusal to reconsider, I sent a protesting memo to Jack Warner, as did Mike Curtiz, who favored my ending.

The front office never replied to either of us. The compromise ending remained and, looking at it from this perspective, it seems not to have had much effect on the fate of the film. However, when you've been involved in a screenplay for half a year, you come to regard any unwanted change as of earthshaking importance to be prevented at all costs. Later you discover that the sun is still shining, the earth still turning on its axis, and that little has changed.

When the film was released, we expected some controversy, but I doubt if any of us were prepared for the violence of the reactions, both pro and con. By this time many politicians were making a career of opposing New Deal policies, including recognition of the Soviet Union; with others anticommunism was almost a religion. To these rightist elements, including Russian counterrevolutionary exiles, we had committed the ultimate sin, and their attacks were vitriolic. They sometimes picketed theatres where the film was being shown. More moderate voices accused us of whitewashing the Soviet Union. Among these were Professor John Dewey, a prominent educator at Columbia University, and Suzanne LaFollette, editor of various magazines and a cousin of the progressive senator from Wisconsin. They catalogued what they considered the film's faults in a long article in *The New York Times*, but the newspaper reviews were generally favorable, with some reservations.

No doubt some of the criticism was justified. We had weighted the picture heavily on the positive side of Soviet accomplishments, since in our opinion the negative aspects had been amply publicized in our press ever since the revolution. Some of the scenes, such as the seizure of suspected conspirators against the regime, had the nightmare quality of a reign of terror—which was decidedly not "whitewashing." Whether we should have given more footage to the shortcomings of the Soviet system is an open question. We were venturing into new territory for feature films with no precedent to guide us.

Much of the criticism of the picture centered on our treatment of the Moscow trials, still controversial to this day, even in Russia. Were some, or all, of the defendants guilty of a conspiracy with the Nazis to open the Ukraine to the German armies, or were they the innocent victims of a Stalinist purge? I don't pretend to know for certain. In the screenplay I used the exact words of Bukharin, Radek, and other leading defendants as they spoke them in the courtroom and as Ambassador Davies recorded them. If they were "brainwashed," as is often claimed, it was a most expert job, since theirs were not the kind of formally worded confessions police extract from their prisoners. Their statements read like admissions of guilt for which they were sincerely penitent. Either they were telling the truth or they were superb actors in a drama directed from behind the scenes. I doubt if we will ever be certain of the answer, which is buried in the hearts of dead men.

What was the outcome as far as we, the makers of the film, were concerned? Controversy feeds the box office; Warners emerged with a moderate financial success and added prestige for daring such a controversial subject. Curtiz said with feeling, "I make no more social pictures," and went back to westerns, in which there is no doubt as to the good guys and bad guys. Mr. Davies was generous in his praise of the film and took a print to Russia, where he showed it to Stalin, Molotov, and other members of the Presidium in the Kremlin's projection room. Apparently the Soviet leaders were surprised and pleased that a film on this subject was made and shown in the United States.

However, fashions change in politics as they do in manners and morals; *Mission to Moscow* is a prime example. The film, patriotic in the forties, became subversive in the fifties, which caused the embarrassed Warners to bury it deep in their studio vaults. During this same postwar period, the picture was shown all over the Soviet Union. Then, when Stalin fell into disrepute, the Soviets stopped showing the film, since he appeared in one of the scenes. And recently, in celebration of détente between the two countries, *Mission* was dug out of its vaults and given a gala reopening in Washington under the auspices of the American Film Society!

EARTH AND HIGH HEAVEN

Although we had not lived together for some years, my first wife and I were still not officially divorced. Since at the time California divorce laws required the passage of a year before remarriage, Anne and I drove with two friends to Yuma, Arizona, for what, in movie terms, might be called a "packaged wedding." Yuma grinds out marriages the way Detroit turns out cars, some of them defective. Since the town is tucked away close to the Mexican border, a day's drive from Los Angeles, most of the ceremonies are performed at night, *performed* being the telling word. The main street is theatrically lit with lofty neon signs advertising its marital wares—license, minister, appropriate bridal music, witnesses if you need them, beds if you want them, even rice throwers—all in one "hallowed hall."

We chose one of the less garish "factories," where we were

greeted by an eager middle-aged man and his smiling wife. The man was the license clerk and the woman turned out to be the minister. Another lady, who must have weighed three hundred pounds, belted out the wedding march, putting every pound into each strident note. Up to now the female minister (of what sect I have no idea) had spoken to us in normal tones, but once the ceremony started, she assumed a high, ministerial voice, almost a chant. We managed to last out the ceremony until the final "I dos" gave us blessed relief.

Afterward the four of us went to a nearby bar to purify ourselves with dry martinis, which Anne insisted were "holy water" in keeping with Yuma's bizarre marital rites. Some years later when it was time to take up our first option, being unsure of our marital status in the other forty-seven states, we had another ceremony, with Anne's mother in attendance to be certain that her daughter was really married.

We rented a house on Toluca Lake in North Hollywood within walking distance of the Warners studio. Our son, Peter, was born in 1947 and a clownish boxer dog, Bobo, completed the household. Across from us was the Lakeside Club where many celebrities, such as Bob Hope and Bing Crosby, played golf. Bobo used to swim the lake, scamper to the eighteenth green, and scoop up the golf balls of approaching players. The balls clamped in his ample chops, Bobo would swim back and proudly present us with his loot. Since big wagers were often at stake among the competing players, Bobo's antics didn't endear us to the club celebrities.

With *Mission to Moscow* now in circulation, our lives settled into a pleasant routine. I continued to write for Warner Brothers and Anne did the screenplay for a low-budget picture which opened a small rift in the Hays office censorship. It became the first Hollywood film in which an act of adultery was allowed without punishment for the lovers. How she convinced Mr. Breen, in charge of the Hays office and a tough man on questions of sexual morality, I'll never know. Perhaps the secret is in her oblique approach, avoiding a direct confrontation, findings ways by indirection, sometimes by humor, to accomplish what she has in mind. Looking back on this tranquil period, I realize we took our good fortune for granted as though it was ours by right to be continued indefinitely. Instead, it turned out to be another idyllic interlude—a calm before the storm that would eventually submerge our careers, at least for a time, and send us into a five-year exile.

Although I wrote the screenplays for several more Warners pictures, including *Three Strangers* with Peter Lorre and Geraldine Fitzgerald, it was becoming clear in the material they were submitting to their writers that the front office was carefully avoiding the kind of significant themes that had made their pictures so relevant to the thirties and forties. Since I had offers from other studios, I asked to be released from my contract, but Warners refused.

At this time, a strike broke out at the studio and the gates were picketed by the back lot employees. One day the studio police were ordered to turn the fire hoses on the pickets. The strike was broken, along with the democratic union which up to then had represented the studio employees. A company-favored union moved in to take its place, much as happened in the California grape and wine industry.

During the strike a wire protesting the fire hosing was sent to Jack Warner. When he saw my name on the telegram, he was furious, regarding my participation as a betrayal of the studio that had done so much for my career. As a consequence, he was now willing to grant my release, but not without my paying the studio a substantial sum of money.

Almost immediately I was offered an assignment by Samuel Goldwyn. He had bought *Earth and High Heaven,* a popular novel by the Canadian authoress Gwethalyn Graham. Since it was to be the first picture on the theme of anti-Semitism, Goldwyn wanted Gregory Peck and Joan Fontaine for the leads, both at the height of their popularity, to enhance the film's commercial prospects. They were interested and though no contracts had been signed, it seemed like a going project. I liked the novel, a tender love story complicated by the racial prejudice of the girl's family and community, and I agreed to do the screenplay.

Having heard the usual droll stories about the legendary Mr. Goldwyn, I was eager to meet him. But no contact was made my first month at the studio while I was working on a story treatment. After it was finished, his secretary called to make an appointment.

When I entered his office he remained seated behind his desk, a tall, gaunt, balding, rather austere figure. Dispensing with all formalities, he motioned me to a chair in front of his desk. But he didn't look at me; his eyes remained on a script in his hands, which I assumed to be my treatment. Seconds passed without a word being spoken. Judging from his grave expression, I felt he had either just received bad news or, more likely, was about to impart some. I waited.

Finally he looked up. "I read your treatment. I have to tell you what I think."

"Yes, Mr. Goldwyn."

"Your opening is not as good as the book. I don't know why you didn't follow the book."

I had my reasons but decided first to hear him out.

"And the scene in the café where the lovers meet . . ." He didn't finish the sentence. He didn't need to. The dejected way he shook his head spoke volumes.

"You left out some of the best scenes in the book. I paid a hundred thousand dollars for that book and you throw away my money."

I still waited. Maybe he would like *something*.

"And the ending. The audience would resent it. I resented it."

He closed the script, tossed it aside, looked at me, frowning as though challenging me to defend my approach. But by this time I felt his criticism was so sweeping that any argument to support my point of view would be hopeless.

"I'm sorry, Mr. Goldwyn. That's the way I see the story on the screen. But it's your property and you have a right to have it done your way. I suggest you find another writer."

Goldwyn stared at me with curiosity, then shook his head as though my reaction was beyond his comprehension.

"You writers. So sensitive. Here I am trying to tell you how much I like your treatment!"

Mr. Goldwyn had lived up to his reputation. I remained on the project, completing the first and second drafts of the screenplay. Despite his idiosyncrasies, Samuel Goldwyn was a good producer. He was willing to spend any amount of time and money to get what he wanted on the screen.

To ensure authenticity, he paid Anne's and my expenses to visit Miss Graham in Montreal. A frank, intelligent woman, she revealed that *Earth and High Heaven* was the story of her own love affair. So that we could absorb the atmosphere, she guided us to all the homes, streets, parks, and cafés where the incidents in the book took place. A cameraman, also sent by Goldwyn, photographed us in the actual settings of the story for purposes of publicity.

For reasons that had nothing to do with the story or the screenplay, the picture was never made. Samuel Goldwyn and Darryl Zanuck were friends. They both loved the game of croquet and played on each other's courts. But in matters of business, I discovered, friendship is no deterrent to doing the other fellow in. Zanuck had also become interested in producing a film on the subject of anti-Semitism. He bought *Gentleman's Agreement,* a gimmicky "pretend to be a Jew" story unlike *Earth and High Heaven,* in which the male lead was actually a Jew. It was Goldwyn's misfortune that Zanuck had a contractual hold on Gregory Peck for one picture. He exercised his right and took Peck practically from under our camera. Goldwyn didn't want to risk a second film on the same theme, particularly since he had lost his male star. Our project was shelved, and *Gentleman's Agreement,* for daring to treat a taboo subject, received that year's Academy Award.

Even after the film had been abandoned, Goldwyn seemed to want me to remain at his studio. He asked me to confer with Robert Sherwood, who was working on *The Best Years of Our Lives*. Sherwood and I talked, but he was perfectly capable of doing the screenplay by himself and my contribution was negligible.

By this time my salary had risen to the crazy figure of three thousand dollars a week, more than I or anyone else was worth. So far I had received about seventy-five thousand from the studio on a project that had never materialized. Feeling guilty, I made an appointment to see Goldwyn.

He was in an amiable mood. "Well, what can I do for you?"

"Mr. Goldwyn, you've done enough. I don't think you should pay me any more salary."

Instead of being pleased, or at least relieved, as I had expected, Mr. Goldwyn looked pained.

"For Chrissake, you think maybe I can't afford it?"

"That's not the point. I don't think I'm earning it."

"That's for me to decide, not you."

"Look, Mr. Goldwyn, I'll stay around if I can do anything for you. Just don't pay me any more money."

He looked at me incredulously. "You know, Koch, with funny ideas like yours, I don't think you'll last very long in Hollywood."

Goldwyn was right, but for reasons neither of us at the time suspected.

NO SAD SONGS FOR ME

My next assignment was at Columbia Pictures, where producer
Buddy Adler offered me free rein to create what was almost an
original story from a novel the studio had purchased titled *No
Sad Songs for Me*. It had a central idea that appealed to me—a
woman in her late thirties, happily married and the mother of a
nine-year-old girl, learns from her doctor that she has terminal
cancer, faces the inevitable, and puts her house in order in the
brief time allotted her.

None of us asked for life, but once it is bestowed on us, we
may question why it can be so capriciously taken away. And
there is no reliable authority from whom we can demand an
answer. Each of us must find his own reason for his circumscribed existence and, consciously or unconsciously, when this

time span is compressed into six months with no chance of a reprieve, human nature is put to its ultimate test.

A person may respond in any number of ways. He may drown his knowledge in liquor or drugs. Or he may find solace in the promises of one or another organized religion. Another course is to beat death to the punch, so to speak, by taking one's own life. Since in this matter, we're all on our own, no one has the right to fault any of these alternatives. . . . However, the choice that the heroine made in *No Sad Songs* seems to me the most gallant. She laid her stake on life itself, even though she was down to the last few chips. She lived and died in accord with the poetic vision of Gibran's Prophet when he said, "You would know the secret of death? But how shall you find it unless you seek it in the heart of life?"

Knowing full well the hazards of dealing with this kind of subject matter for the screen, I decided to chance it. Unless it was understated and played with the utmost simplicity, it could easily degenerate into soap opera, evoking cheap tears instead of the catharsis of tragedy.

While I had no previous experience with the Columbia studio, I had heard lurid tales about its production head, Harry Cohn, that were not exactly reassuring. Yet Columbia had made some fine pictures (as well as some very bad ones) under his auspices. In the course of my association with him, I found Cohn a much more complex man than the gossip pictured him. On his desk he kept a leather-thonged policeman's club. During story conferences he would occasionally pick up the club and give it a few twirls to remind you who was boss. Although he could be rude and even sadistic to his close associates, he had respect for writers, especially those who were not dependent on him. Since I was in this category, our relations throughout, with one exception, were cordial.

It was soon evident to me that behind his tough exterior, Harry Cohn was an extremely vulnerable man, unsure of himself in both his professional and personal life. In the movie world the man on top stays there only as long as his pictures make money. A series of failures can unseat him no matter how successful he has been in the past. Waiting in the background for him to falter are ambitious aspirants for his job. This was particularly true at Columbia, where much of the corporate stock was controlled by its eastern officers, some of them hostile to Cohn.

At this time I met Mrs. Cohn at a friend's house in Beverly Hills. She was an attractive, sophisticated woman a good deal younger than her husband. In the course of the evening, she was called to the phone. She came back, announcing casually, "Harry checking up on me."

Our hosts, old friends of the Cohns, took this as a matter of course, but Mrs. Cohn, noticing my puzzled expression, laughed. "He always does."

"But why?" I couldn't resist the question.

"He wants to know where I am and with whom."

Since she was my dinner partner for the evening, I must have passed the "safe escort" test.

I think Mrs. Cohn rather enjoyed her husband's protective measures because she elaborated for my benefit. "He has a guard at the gate checking when I go out and what time I return."

The results of concentrated wealth and power appear to be the opposite of what they are presumed to achieve—security and tranquillity. It seems a high price to pay for the privileges and possessions belonging to a man in his position.

The tycoons who dominated Hollywood in the first half of the century were adventurers operating in a competitive jungle. They might socialize together, but during business hours they were ready to cut each other's throats, along with anyone else's, when they felt their interests threatened or their authority challenged. Yet despite their questionable ethics and their despotic methods, these men possessed certain attributes lacking in those who hold the purse strings in filmmaking today. Gamblers by nature, they were willing to take risks and make personal decisions. At the present time it would be difficult to find a movie executive who could say on his own, "I like the story, make it." Instead, the decision would filter through committees of distributors, bankers, lawyers, agents, and it may very well eventually be a computer that gives the final "yes" or "no."

Harry Cohn took what he knew was a financial risk for reasons that the computer watcher of today would not understand; the courageous way one woman met her fate suggests the human potential for nobility, and apparently this touched some responsive chord in Cohn that had nothing to do with his business instincts.

Not that the path from the conception of the film to its execution was a smooth one. As usual it was an obstacle course right down to the finish line. After several revisions, my screenplay was accepted by Cohn and his associate producer, Buddy Adler. However, two vital factors had to be solved before there could be a production: finding a female star with the stature for a tragic role and finding a sensitive and sympathetic director.

For years Harry Cohn and other studio heads had been trying to lure Margaret Sullavan away from the stage and back to films, but up to now, she had turned down every offer. We all agreed she possessed the acting ability and personal attributes needed for the role. Since I was going east, Cohn asked me to take a script to her. She read it immediately and called me on the phone. Her answer was as direct as she was as a person. "I like it and I'll do it. Tell Harry to get in touch with my agent."

With this hurdle cleared, I went back to Hollywood in high spirits. Then the blow fell from an unexpected quarter. During my absence Cohn had given my script to Sam Wood with the hope of getting him to direct. Wood was a very capable director with pictures to his credit that were both commercially successful and critically acclaimed. However, he, along with John Wayne, had organized a small but powerful group of film people calling themselves the Motion Picture Alliance for the Preservation of American Ideals. Unfortunately, the "American ideals"

they sought to preserve were fanatically reactionary and jingoistic. To them any social reform that challenged the interests of a
privileged class was "Communist" or "Communist-inspired." The
Soviet Union or socialism in any form were anathema to them,
and since I had done the screenplay for *Mission to Moscow,* I
was marked as an enemy. Wood wanted to direct *No Sad Songs*
but not if "that Communist bastard" had anything to do with it.
He took it upon himself to hire a writer of his political persuasion,
and working together they turned out a new screenplay in several
weeks.

Cohn was in a quandary. He didn't like their screenplay but he
had great respect for Wood's directorial ability. Margaret Sullavan solved his dilemma. When she arrived in Hollywood, she was
given the new script to read. She went to Cohn and told him this
wasn't the screenplay submitted to her in New York, and under
no circumstances would she do the picture unless the original
script was restored.

Wood was furious. He went to Miss Sullavan and argued with
her, but she was not impressed with either his defense of the new
script or his attack on me and my screenplay. I never read the
substitute script, but a producer at the studio later told me that
Wood had turned the story into a political diatribe. How he managed to make a political issue of a woman dying of cancer I can't
imagine. Possibly the malignant tissue was composed of Communist cells implanted by a secret Soviet agent.

After that last-minute save, Rudolph Mate became the director.
A leading cinematographer, he resisted the temptation to show
off his camera virtuosity and shot the film with honesty and fidelity to the human values. Margaret Sullavan played the tragic
heroine without once striking a false or sentimental note. She
even made credible her last act of preparing the way for her suc-
cessor, a girl who worked for her husband and was in love with
him, to take her place as his wife and mother of their child. If
this sounds like the stuff of soap opera, much of the preventive
credit must go to Miss Sullavan's sensitive performance.

We avoided the cliché deathbed scene or any morbid dwelling on her physical death. Instead, she was in Mexico on a last vacation with her husband, who now knew of her fatal illness. The other woman, played by another fine actress, Viveca Lindfors, was giving a piano lesson to the child when the telephone rang. The camera moved in close on the black phone, magnified in its size and its import. Viveca answered the phone and the expression on her face told us all we needed to know. The picture ended with the piano lesson resuming on a theme from Brahms's First Symphony, quietly at first, then an orchestra taking over and building in a triumphant crescendo.

A sneak preview is an institution that only Hollywood could have invented. The producer, director, the studio executives, and sometimes the writer are picked up by chauffeur-driven limousines to be taken to an unknown destination. Only the top brass know where the preview is to take place. The limousines are black, the mood of their occupants solemn. One has a feeling he is being taken to a funeral, and often the result is not too different. If the audience reaction is so bad that the case is considered hopeless, the film may be laid to rest in the studio archives. Or if the reaction is mixed, it may be given a probationary run without the benefit of heavy advance publicity (which is usually a slow death) and, at least today, a quick release to television to recoup its costs.

The preview of *No Sad Songs for Me* was held in Pasadena with more than the usual tension on our part. How would the audience react to a film that dealt frankly with a subject evoking universal dread? At the final fade-out, the preview audience remained in their seats. There was complete silence for ten seconds before they released their emotions in sustained applause. It was the response we had hoped for; *No Sad Songs* had passed the test. Its success was confirmed when Radio City Music Hall booked the picture, the first departure in its history from what is known in the trade as strictly entertainment films.

After the preview, about eleven o'clock, we were told to come

to Harry Cohn's office. It was on this occasion that I had my first
brush with Cohn. The meeting was attended by those directly
connected with the production, together with the department
heads and assistants. The preview cards, filled out by members
of the audience, were read aloud by one of the assistants. They
were highly laudatory, all but one that simply read, "Lousy." It
seems that this card invariably turns up; its author must go from
preview to preview just to make his comment. Anyway, it was a
minority opinion and made little impression. Elated by the re-
sponses, Cohn, billy club in hand, swept his eyes over the gathering.

"Well, any of you got suggestions before we make final prints?"

There was something in his tone that warned us that we had
better not have any because the film was perfect and any damn
fool would know it from the preview cards.

It turned out there was only one "damn fool." My objection
was very minor. I didn't like the arbitrary cut in the outdoor
scene, which stopped just short of an embrace between the husband and his girl assistant, an embrace that implied an actual
affair instead of a mere flirtation. To me it was blurring something
the audience had a right to know. After I made the suggestion,
there was complete silence in the room. Everyone looked at me
as though I had spoken my last words before being led to the
electric chair.

For several moments Cohn said nothing, just glared at me.
Then he launched into a fifteen-minute lecture on "taste." Didn't
I realize how much the audience would resent a man having an
affair when his wife was dying of cancer? I pointed out that the
husband didn't know, his wife and her doctor having kept her
terminal illness a secret. Cohn then went into a long eulogy of
the picture right down to the amount of tears shed by members
of his household—the butler, chauffeur, gardener, and various
maids—when he showed it in his home. He seemed to forget that
I had something to do with the picture he was so vigorously
defending. Actually I was as gratified by the reception of *No Sad*

Songs as he was. All I wanted was to put back a few feet of film that were already shot. However, it was Columbia's film, not mine, and the footage was never restored.

Today the same situation might well have been reversed. The average producer would undoubtedly ask me to write and the director to photograph the affair in all its anatomical details. Within the last year I've seen sexual intercourse simulated in bed, on the floor, in the rain, in snow, under water, and even on top of a fence. It seems inevitable that the possible variations of places and positions will soon be exhausted.

Because of the need to compress experience into representative images, the film medium is more akin to poetry than prose, evoking a deeper response by what is implicit in an act than by its literal depiction. The touch of hands can be more sensuous than the culminating sexual act. It seems to me that the filmmaker's art is to involve the audience in the emotions and sensations of the participants rather than in their sexual techniques, unless, of course, the purpose is to instruct the uninitiated—an intent I very much doubt is in the minds of commercial filmmakers.

Harry Cohn's pique with me was of very short duration. A few weeks later he asked me to write a story and screenplay on the subject of another disease. It was, and still is, a hallowed custom in Hollywood to follow a success with another picture as much like it as possible, creating, if all goes well, a trend. In each case the follow-up film has to be more adventurous in its subject or treatment to justify its existence. It wasn't easy to think of a disease with a worse reputation than cancer, but Columbia came up with one—leprosy.

WHO WALK ALONE

I had no wish to be typed as a writer of stories about diseases any more than as one whose specialty was Martians. However, I sensed from the little I knew about it that the subject of leprosy could have social implications that would justify its use as screen material. Since biblical times lepers have been outcasts, untouchables, more isolated and discriminated against than Jews, blacks, Indians, or any oppressed group. Lepers could be considered the ultimate minority, symbolic of all the others.

Since Anne was occupied with our somewhat obstreperous three-year-old son, I asked the studio to have Anne Taylor work with me on the project. Anne was the mutual friend who had arranged our original meeting on *Mission to Moscow,* my erstwhile secretary on the Mercury programs, and now an established screenwriter. She had what John Houseman called a "mousetrap

mind." If he meant by that "sharp," I could agree with him—
quick to pounce on what might be useful in plot construction, a
valuable asset in dealing with a subject matter so far removed
from our previous experience.

Together with William Dozier, our associate producer, we set
off for Carville, Louisiana, where the only leprosarium in America
is situated. Its location was indicative of society's attitude toward
the disease. About thirty miles north of New Orleans, the fenced-
in compound was surrounded on three sides by a swamp, snake-
and alligator-infested, and on the fourth by the Mississippi River.
Since the disease is endemic to the tropics, the hot, sultry atmosphere of Carville was hardly a suitable environment for treating
its victims.

I don't know what my two associates were thinking, but I'll
confess to some apprehensions and misgivings when we were admitted through the well-guarded gates into a world so alien to
our own that it might have been on some distant planet. That
evening the head doctor called an assembly of the patients to
give us an opportunity to explain the purpose of our visit. I'll
never forget my first sight of this gathering. Instead of seeing
four hundred different persons I had the startling impression I
was looking at one person multiplied by four hundred. One of the
early manifestations of leprosy, or Hansen's disease as they preferred to call it, is a widening and flattening of the features, giving the victims a leonine expression that accounts for facial simi-
larities.

Since the doctors had warned us about the extreme sensitivity
of the patients, we assured them that we had no intention of
exploiting the sensational aspects of their malady for commercial
purposes. Rather, we hoped our film would help to dissipate some
of the existing prejudices and ancient superstitions connected
with the disease. They listened to us attentively, but I had a feeling from their questions that they were reserving judgment. After
all, we were "Hollywood characters"—how did they know they
could trust us? Since we planned to shoot the film in semidocu-

mentary style right there in the compound, it was obvious we had
to have their cooperation. Our speeches hadn't achieved it; some
other method must be found.

During the first couple of days we were given a complete tour
of the colony, including the isolated compound where we saw
the grotesque disfigurements that made leprosy the most dreaded
name in our vocabulary of diseases. Faces without features, hands
without fingers, minds bereft of reason, human beings reduced to
bundles of decaying flesh. Most of these were old people stricken
by the disease before the advent of sulfa drugs.

In recent years these drugs have minimized the ravages of the
disease. Treated in time, leprosy can be arrested and made non-
contagious in over 90 percent of the cases. Since there was a
question of which method of administering the drug was more
beneficial, the patients were divided into two groupings, each to
be a control to the other. Every morning all the inmates who
were ambulatory formed double lines, one to take the prescribed
dose orally, the other by hypodermic injection. In time it became
a game among the patients to see which group could arrest the
disease more quickly. The good-natured competition even produced two rival baseball teams—the "oralers" and the "injectors."
It was a medical requirement that a patient pass ten consecutive
immunity checks spaced over a period of time before he or she
could be released from the colony. One can imagine the suspense
of an inmate who had passed eight or nine tests and was facing
the critical tenth.

The resident doctors were cooperative, and it appeared to us
that, within the limits of their facilities, they did all they could
to make life bearable for the colony's enforced inhabitants. More
difficult to cope with than the disease itself, the doctors told us,
was the ignorant and prejudiced attitude of society toward the
sufferers, even after they had been released as no longer contagious. This, Anne and I quickly decided, would be the focal point
of our story, which would widen its significance in relating to all
minorities.

In the course of our tour of the grounds, one of the doctors showed us the "hole in the fence," an obscure opening tunneled by the inmates. This was the escape valve used by some of the patients when the claustrophobic pressures became too great. Actually, they were prohibited by law from leaving the compound until officially discharged, but the marine authorities compassionately looked the other way as far as this breach was concerned. The patients would slip out for part of a day to attend a movie or a baseball game in New Orleans or some neighboring town. Then there were special occasions when large numbers of the inmates would go through the fence to the adjacent Mississippi levee for a few evening hours of diversion when their black neighbors provided a fish fry, enlivened by jazz music and dancing. During these festive outings the patients would take up a collection for their impoverished hosts, always on the pretext "to pay for a new roof on their church." Apparently the church, if it existed, never got its roof, but no one seemed to mind. The nearby blacks were an exception to the taboo imposed by the community at large, evidently not sharing the superstitious dread of the disease. It was a classical case of one oppressed minority relating sympathetically to another, an observation we noted for our story.

After a few days Bill Dozier returned to the studio, leaving Anne Taylor and me to complete the research. So far we had a general picture of life in the colony and had absorbed some of its atmosphere. But the knowledge we had gained was all from the doctors' point of view, not from that of the patients. We needed in some way to know how they felt about their circumscribed existence. Assured by the doctors that leprosy was not contagious except by "long and intimate contact," such as between mother and child or husband and wife, we resolved to break down the barriers by living with the patients as much as possible, only returning to our rooms in the doctors' quarters at night. We had noticed that there were several key people among the inmates. One was a handsome man in his late forties, blinded by the disease. A devoted fellow patient had attached himself to this per-

son, guiding him from place to place although the blind man
could manage quite well by the use of his cane and what seemed
like some sort of extrasensory perception. By virtue of his character and intelligence, he was the acknowledged leader and
spokesman for the inhabitants of the colony.

Next in influence were a young Filipino woman who had been
a guerrilla fighter against the Japanese invaders of her country,
and her lover, an American GI who had caught the disease in the
Philippines. The sexual freedom practiced today was anticipated
years ago in this isolated community. While there were separate
male and female dormitories, no one paid any attention to the
distinction. The doctors told us that when a new patient arrived,
the whole population was restless until he or she had chosen a
lover. Many of the patients had husbands or wives on the outside,
but the leper colony was a world apart in which intramural mat-
ings were an accepted way of life. Only when one or another of
the partners was discharged did the "marriage" end.

When we first appeared in their dining room, taking our seats
with the patients, they regarded us with some surprise. While
they were polite, answering our questions, they were still on their
guard. Obviously we were being watched and tested. We knew
that sooner or later there would be a decision whether to accept
us, and we suspected that the blind man would tip the scales. He
made a point of spending time with us and we had the impression that his observation of us was more penetrating than that of
a person with normal sight.

On the second day we were invited to the room occupied by
the Filipino girl and her American lover. We looked on this as a
breakthrough. By going to their room we could demonstrate that
we didn't share the conventional superstitious attitude toward
their disease.

During those several hours, the barriers went down. They were
bright young people, their wits sharpened by the intensity of
their experiences. Like everyone, they were curious about Hollywood and moviemaking. Then the conversation drifted to politics

and, to their delight, they found that we shared their more or less radical political views. The blind man joined us later, and before long we had become friends.

The next day when we appeared in the dining room, the whole atmosphere had changed. Everyone wanted to talk with us and contribute to the picture in some way. There was a small, rough golf course in the compound, and each afternoon I played golf with the ex-GI and two other patients. They were excellent golfers who played every day.

All during this time, we were making notes, with enough stories being showered on us for a dozen films. One account of how the disease was discovered gave us an idea for the opening sequence. The young man was working on a farm when the barn caught fire. In the course of rescuing animals and equipment, his hands were severely burned. But he only realized this by the blisters that appeared on his palms a short time later. He had absolutely no pain from the burn. A numbness of some part of the body is one of the revealing symptoms of the disease. After various medical examinations one doctor finally diagnosed it as leprosy.

In many instances the diagnosis involves the victim in a dilemma. Incarceration in a leper colony is not something the average person can face with equanimity. What are the alternatives? He can move from the place where his affliction is known and try to start a new life among strangers. Wherever he goes, however, he will accumulate guilt from the fear of spreading the contagion. Since failure to report the disease is breaking the law, he becomes a fugitive. Moreover, the malady doesn't get better by itself. By not submitting to a course of treatment, he can worsen his illness to the point where its grotesque disfigurements become visible. Usually, sooner or later, he makes the hard decision and becomes a patient at Carville.

In some ways the atmosphere of a leprosarium brought to mind Thomas Mann's novel *The Magic Mountain*, depicting life in a tubercular sanitarium. Both diseases are accompanied by variations in the fever chart. Although the temperature rise is usually slight, the feverishness is reflected psychologically in the behavior of the patient. Emotions are more volatile, reactions are disproportionate to the stimuli, life is lived on a higher key. This is true not only in the patient's sex life but also in his intense preoccupation with the attitudes of the outside world toward his affliction.

Like other oppressed minorities, the inmates of Carville had their own underground communication system. Even in their extreme isolation they were able to follow the fortunes and misfortunes of former patients who had been discharged. They knew how many were able to secure jobs, how they were received by their families and friends, in short, to what extent the superstitious fear of the disease prevented them from living a normal life. There were instances where discharged patients returned to the colony, unable to cope with the pressures and prejudices they encountered. Tempers might flare among themselves, but in relation to the outside world they were a united fraternity.

Ironically, the only segregation in the colony was practiced in the two chapels, one Catholic, the other Protestant. Whites occupied one side of the aisle, blacks the other. Although they could eat together and sleep together, they couldn't worship together. I should make it clear that I'm reporting a condition that existed when I was there over twenty years ago, and I'm certain that this form of ecclesiastic segregation is no longer practiced even in the Deep South.

By the time we left Carville, we had an outline of what we felt would make a fascinating and significant film. We arrived at the studio eager to obtain the approval of Harry Cohn so that we could start on the screenplay. A week passed, then another. When I called, Mr. Cohn was always busy. I couldn't get through to him past his barrier of secretaries. Nor could Bill Dozier, our associate producer. I was being paid a high salary for doing nothing, and I wasn't happy.

Finally one of his assistants broke the news to me that Mr. Cohn was dropping the project. A film dealing with a disease, made by another company, had just failed.

"But why wouldn't he see me?"

The assistant grinned. "He thought you might be contagious."

LETTER FROM
AN UNKNOWN WOMAN

What interests me most as a dramatist is human behavior under stress, but I believe that a story, to possess validity, must show the interplay between its characters and their environment. No story can exist in a vacuum, not even a love story as romantic and nostalgic as *Letter from an Unknown Woman*. Critics such as Andrew Sarris of the *Village Voice* and Richard Corliss, editor of *Film Comment,* have rated the picture high in their rankings of cinematic art and, throwing modesty to the winds, I am inclined to agree with them. Perhaps my immodest appraisal is tempered by the fact that I had the most talented producer, director, and cast to be found anywhere in the movie world.

During Hollywood's heyday most film productions were put together as haphazardly as the combinations that turn up on a roll of dice. Occasionally the lucky number came up. I was one

of the few American writers with the good fortune to have
worked with the late Max Ophuls. Although few of his European
films had reached America, he had already acquired a European
reputation as a sensitive artist. Today, a decade and more after
his death, he is one of the directors most revered by filmmakers
and critics on both continents.

I met Max in the early forties at the home of a friend. With his
wife and school-age son, he had escaped from occupied France
to Switzerland one step ahead of the advancing Germans. After
several months he and his family managed to obtain passage to
this country, joining the swelling number of refugee artists centered in New York and Hollywood. In a burst of philanthropic
zeal the major movie studios opened their gates to these politically displaced writers, directors, and actors, putting many of
them on salary. Having made the gesture, however, they did
little to make use of their talents.

At the time I met Max he had neither work nor charity and was
living precariously on the last of what funds he had been able to
salvage from Europe. He was like a baldish Peter Lorre, with the
same heavy-lidded, wide-set eyes and the same impish sense of
humor. Our rapport was immediate. In the first hour of our meeting I knew that I wanted to work with him on a film. It wasn't
his reputation, since I was hardly aware of his European career.
Max was not lacking in self-confidence, but he didn't look upon
film narcissistically as a public mirror to display his virtuosity. He
had a deep respect for what others contributed and, particularly,
for the basic content of the screenplay, a quality understandably
endearing to a writer. This may come as a surprise to some critics
who praise Max, and justly, as a superb stylist, but from my observation, his style was invariably related to content, never at its
expense.

One of his attributes that impressed me was his sensitivity to
English words, since English was not his native language and he
spoke it brokenly with little regard for grammatical construction.
Nevertheless, his ear was attuned to the most delicate nuances,

and he was never satisfied with a word or a line of dialogue until it expressed the precise shade of meaning needed to convey the idea or emotion.

At times I suspected that he clung to certain verbal eccentricities because they enhanced his special brand of humor. One day we were going to the studio in his old, battered car. Max was a terrible driver: he couldn't keep his mind—or his car—on the road. Fortunately, he never went fast, so his accidents, while numerous, were never serious. On this occasion he was tailgating another car which slowed down without Max noticing, and we collided with its rear. Max was out of his seat in an instant, and after a brief survey of the other car, he doffed his little Tyrolean hat to its occupants and blithely announced, "It makes no never mind." The other driver was apparently so intrigued with Max's quaint manners and expression that he didn't climb out to look at his bent bumper. Off we went, scot-free of all the bothersome details of exchanging names, addresses, and insurance agents.

Before long, Anne and I became close friends with Max and his family, which included his wife, Hilde, a handsome woman in her forties who had been a leading German actress; Marcel, his talented teen-age son and now the illustrious and controversial director of social documentaries; and Max's attractive young mistress, a refugee painter from Nazi Germany. Like other displaced Europeans, Max had transplanted his continental sexual habits to America, dividing his time equitably between the two ménages. Since Americans are not adept at this sort of thing, Max undertook to instruct me on some of the finer points. One of his rules that I recall is that cut flowers are properly sent to one's mistress as they are perishable, whereas a plant, being more durable and therefore more economical, is the correct choice for one's wife. Although delicacy required that his wife and mistress be kept separately, we were part of the intimate circle that included both.

Two years passed before there was an opportunity to work with Max. It came about by accident. John Houseman came to

see us on the desert outside Palm Springs where we were then
living. He brought with him a short story by Stefan Zweig entitled "Letter from an Unknown Woman," which he wanted me
to dramatize for the screen. He had been asked to produce the
picture by Joan Fontaine and William Dozier, then husband and
wife, who had formed their own company within the framework
of Universal Studios. The tragic story, written in Zweig's lyrical
prose, was in the form of a letter from a woman on her deathbed
to the bon vivant musician she had loved from girlhood and with
whom she finally had a brief affair, only to discover in later years
that she was one of many and that he didn't even remember her
name.

At first reading I was not impressed with the story as picture
material. It was entirely subjective with only fragmentary incidents. Besides, it was in the highly charged romantic tradition of
Vienna at the turn of the century, definitely not the kind of story
Hollywood did well. Although I had respect for Houseman's
taste, I foresaw the danger of sentimentality, a so-called woman's
picture awash with tears. Then I thought of Max Ophuls. Possibly
he could bring it off, as he, like Zweig, was steeped in the romantic tradition. The upshot was that I agreed to write the screenplay if the studio would accept Max as the director.

Fortunately, Houseman had seen *Liebelei*, Max's most admired
European film, an exquisite piece of romantic nostalgia, also set
in Vienna. He agreed that Max was ideal for *Letter from an Unknown Woman*, but he had to sell the idea of a foreign director
to Joan and Bill Dozier, who in turn had to convince the Universal executives. Since Joan Fontaine was then their most important star, Dozier was able to obtain their reluctant consent.

It was my function to plot a story line that would carry the
emotional progression of Zweig's story. Then followed the usual
conferences with Max and Houseman and, after some revisions,
with Joan and Bill Dozier. Everyone had criticisms and suggestions but, happily, no ego problems intruded so that each contribution could be accepted or rejected on its merits. At this stage,

Joan's ideas in relation to the central character of Lisa were especially helpful. She would be on the screen almost constantly and needed playable situations in which to convey her feelings for the musician at the three different periods in which he entered her life. It was a difficult role, starting as the ardent, hero-worshiping girl of fourteen, then the young woman in her twenties when they had the affair, and finally the mature, love-crossed woman of middle age. Joan Fontaine was one of the few actresses capable of making the intensely romantic Lisa a credible character, and I still regard the performance she eventually gave as one of the most brilliant I have ever seen on film.

Up to now Max had made a few suggestions but stayed mostly in the background; he believed the creative process of constructing a dramatic story was in the writer's province. But once I had the first draft screenplay written, he became deeply involved, testing every line of dialogue and every image for period validity and nuances of character. Out of his own memories of Vienna came ideas for new scenes, such as the one in which the lovers appear to be traveling together in a train compartment, gazing out the window at the exotic foreign scenery which turns out to be merely a rotating backdrop in one of the amusement concessions in Vienna's Prater.

In recent years I have read with some bewilderment statements of French film directors identifying their methods with those of Max Ophuls, whom they apparently regard as a precursor of the New Wave. Yet these directors are among the chief exponents of the auteur theory, popularized by *Cahiers du Cinema* and *Sight and Sound*, which holds that a director "authors" a film on the set and later in the cutting rooms with some small assist from a "dialogue writer."

Since this practically dispenses with the screenplay as a basic ingredient in the creative process, it could hardly be further from Max's approach to picture making. No one could be more meticulous in the preparation of a script for its transition to the screen. I don't mean to suggest a slavish rigidity to what was written, since

Max often improvised on the set, but these improvisations were in the nature of refinements, not basic changes in the story line or characterizations.

For the final polishing we went over to Catalina Island off the California coast. Max had a phobia about flying, and this was his first flight. During the half-hour in the air, he sat hunched over, refusing to talk or look out the window, resigned to imminent death. When the plane landed safely, I'm sure to Max it was like a last-minute, unexpected reprieve.

During our stay in Catalina, I recall that Max kept repeating, "This script needs more air." At first I wasn't sure what he meant but I came to realize that "air" referred to atmosphere. In the broadest sense each scene must have a life of its own apart from its dramatic function in the story. And in this area Max was the acknowledged master. No scene that he directed ever existed in a vacuum, and in the case of *Letter from an Unknown Woman* the detail of Viennese life in that period saturated the screen.

One example comes to mind. In the lyrical Prater sequence, the lovers are dancing in a deserted ballroom, oblivious to everything but each other. Since music was an obvious necessity, I had written in shots of a conventional male orchestra playing while Lisa (Joan) and her lover (Louis Jordan) waltzed. Max, recalling that women musicians were often employed in Viennese amusement parks, cast an all-female band. The scene was late at night, the women were desperately tired, and the music they played between swigs of beer was equally tired. The humor of these frowsy women, scraping their violins and wishing to God that these moon-calf lovers would stop dancing so that they could go home, counterpointed the lyrical mood and added period flavor ("air").

Under the supervision of Max and an Austrian technical adviser the sets were so authentically Viennese that few people who saw the film could believe they were built on a Hollywood stage. The shooting under Max's assured direction went smoothly, with all of us—Max, Joan, Dozier, Houseman, and myself—very happy with the daily rushes. Only one incident that took place near the end of the shooting schedule marred the working relationship between the star and the director.

Max was born in Alsace-Lorraine, which is either French or German, depending on which side won the last war. His temperament reflected both national backgrounds. Generally, he seemed much more French than German, but on occasion a Prussian trait was exposed—mostly in regard to women. While shooting a scene, Joan objected to some direction he gave her and Max made the mistake of accusing her of "behaving like a star." Joan walked off the set and stayed off for two days. It took all Houseman's diplomacy to bring her back to finish the picture.

The shooting ended on schedule, a rough cut was made, then a final cut—or one we thought was final. We all felt good about the result and a vacation was in order. Anne and I went east; Max and his family stayed in our house on the desert.

Our departure was a mistake. While we were away, the studio executives came into the projection room with their knives and slashed away at the film to "make it move faster." Since they are mostly occupied with the business end of picture making, this is their one opportunity to be "creative" and to exercise their authority over the film's real creators.

When Max and I returned to the studio, we were told that twenty minutes had been taken out of the film's running time. We ran the reedited print in shocked silence. Then we exploded. Instead of "moving faster," the picture now seemed interminable.

Something we learn from experience is that clock time and screen time have little to do with each other. Two hours in a movie house may seem short while twenty minutes may seem to drag on forever, depending on the extent to which the audience is involved in what is happening on the screen.

Letter from an Unknown Woman, by its nature, required slow pacing and minute attention to evocative detail. What the studio heads had done was to strip much of the flesh from the bones of the story. Since the film had very little plot in the usual sense and its highly romantic premise was difficult to sustain, it would work only if the audience was so caught up in its spell that they were willing to suspend their disbelief for the duration of the show.

I have a theory that any story, however slight, will hold an audience so long as the motivations and actions of its characters are credible in relation to the circumstances surrounding their fictional lives. In its abbreviated version *Letter* had preserved the story incidents but had lost the ambience that gave credible life to its characters. As a result, the film was shorter in actual minutes but, in failing to convince the viewer and hold his interest, it seemed longer.

Houseman agreed with our objections, but it took all his powers of persuasion to keep Max from invading the inner sanctum of Universal's top brass and telling them exactly what he thought of them—which, of course, would only have made them more obdurate. When the Doziers finally threw their weight on our side, we were able to replace the cut footage and reinstate the original version.

However, a film is never safe from tampering until it's "in the can," ready for distribution, and even then it can be so mishandled that it never reaches its intended audience. The sales department of Universal regarded *Letter* as a foreign film, which in those days meant art but no box office. It was tossed on the market with almost no advance advertising and no attempt to publicize its special qualities. Even with good reviews it didn't survive long enough to find its American audience.

By the sheerest accident it was resurrected in Europe. Universal had sold the British rights to a third-rate English distribution chain that did not even have a releasing outlet in London. It happened that one of the editors of the prestigious *Sight and Sound* was visiting a small town where *Letter* was playing. Since the film had not been shown in London and he had never heard of it, he thought it must be one of Hollywood's B pictures. But he had great respect for Joan Fontaine and decided to see it anyway. Apparently he was so impressed by the film and shocked by its treatment that he began a one-man crusade on its behalf. *Sight and Sound* took up the cause and soon it was playing long runs in London and other European capitals. Since then it has become one of the standard revivals at Britain's National Film Theatre.

As for Max, he and his family returned to France, where they were able to reclaim the home the Germans had appropriated. He made a number of films there, the most successful being the first, *La Ronde*, and perhaps the most discussed his last, *Lola Montes*.

When Anne and I arrived in Paris in the early fifties, our former roles were reversed. This time we were the political refugees from McCarthyism in America while Max was the host at the peak of his career. With his shepherding we saw Paris not just as tourists but as part of the French scene. From movie studios to his favorite cafés and restaurants we lived in Max's reflected glory, with the musical theme of *La Ronde* following us as we made the rounds.

Later when we were living in England, Max called me on the phone. He had exciting news. The Thomas Mann heirs were granting him the rights to make a film of *The Magic Mountain*. Would I come back to France as soon as the project was set up and do the screenplay? Another film with Max and a chance to dramatize a great novel! He had my answer in a split second.

A few months later came word of Max's sudden death. We were stunned. We couldn't believe it because we didn't want to believe it. Anne was even angry with him. "He had no right to die."

In later years we again visited Paris but Max was not there and it wasn't the same. To us Max was Paris and Paris was Max.

DECLINE AND FALL

I can remember the exact spot where I was standing in our Toluca Lake house when a radio bulletin announced the death of Franklin Roosevelt; I had an immediate, overwhelming premonition of disaster. In that instant I caught a glimpse of the future and I didn't like what I saw. Try as I might to shake off that foreboding by telling myself that one man's passing couldn't make that much difference, the impression remained with me until eventually the psychic flash, if that is what it was, became objective reality in the events that gradually unfolded.

The men in high positions who celebrated his death that night with parties in their various country clubs knew. They had been waiting impatiently to regain control and were fully prepared with policies and politicians that would liquidate all they could of the New Deal, both in substance and in spirit, foreign and domestic. To implement this about-face, public opinion had to be manipulated and either dissidents had to be brought into line or their views suppressed. Not by accident, the first warning rattle came where dreams (ideas) were generated and widely disseminated. A small, make-believe place, not a city, not even a town, yet bearing a name known all over the world: Hollywood.

Ten filmmakers—writers, directors, producers—were served subpoenas to appear before the House Un-American Activities Committee to face an investigation into their activities and associations. Then nine more were served. I was one of the nine. Because of my nonmembership in the party, I didn't make the first team.

What were the activities for which we were to be investigated? My earliest involvement in organizations listed as subversive was membership in the Hollywood Writers Mobilization, an offshoot of the Screen Writers Guild, formed to volunteer our services to the government's war effort. Drawing on other talents in the movie colony, we provided material and personnel—actors, musicians, cameramen—for shows performed at army camps here and abroad. The entertainments varied from vaudeville skits to symphony orchestra concerts. Even joke books were written and given wide circulation in the interests of boosting army morale. Under Mobilization auspices, John Houseman and I made a documentary film in Riverside, California, titled *The First Tuesday in November,* showing how elections are held in a democratic country as opposed to the Nazi dictatorship we were fighting.

How this organization got on the subversive lists in the postwar era is still a mystery. I can only conclude that an activist group of writers who organize for any purpose is automatically suspect. In later years it was discovered that the phones of Mobilization personnel were being tapped by operatives of one or another of the watchdog committees. This came to light when the library authorities of the University of California at Los Angeles asked that we make a grant to their archives of our voluminous files containing minutes of meetings, literary material produced, artists who participated, and all other records of our varied activities over the war years for the use of future historians. In a telephone conversation between Pauline Lauber, our executive secretary, and the head librarian at UCLA, arrangements were made to deliver the files to the college on a certain day at a specified time. As Ms. Lauber was taken to the hospital for an emergency operation, another Mobilization member transported the files to the campus in his station wagon. Waiting for him at the entrance to the library were a half-dozen policemen!

Apparently they had been alerted by a committee operative who had tapped Ms. Lauber's telephone. Without any explanation the police appropriated the files, the last any of us saw of them. Where they were taken we have never been able to trace. The only clue we have is a report that a research scholar who is writing a book on the McCarthy era purchased part or a facsimile of these files for twenty-five thousand dollars, giving some idea of their historical value.

After the war many of us who had belonged to the Mobilization joined the Arts, Scientists and Professions Council and I became its West Coast chairman. One of our activities was to focus public attention on the plight of oppressed minorities—black, Chicano, Indian—before it became fashionable. We also supported democratic labor unions and sponsored studies and reports on the causes of smog, perhaps one of the earliest concerns for our polluted environment. In the view of the new administration our most flagrant "sin" was our opposition to their Cold War policies. Despite harassment on the streets by police and right-wing groups, members of ASP helped to collect enough signatures to get Henry Wallace on the California ballot as the third-party 1948 presidential candidate, and some of us researched material for his speeches. We were also among the nationwide progressive organizations that initiated the Waldorf Peace Conference. On our board were such "subversive" characters as Albert Einstein, Harlow Shapley, Linus Pauling, Philip Morrison, Paul Robeson, and others of that eminent stature. Needless to say, my connection with ASP was duly recorded by those who were keeping lists.

During recent years I have read controversial articles on whether or not those filmmakers investigated and later blacklisted were guilty of "Stalinism," whatever that word implies. I can only speak from my own experience. I never cared whether my fellow members of these suspect organizations were Democrats, Republicans, socialists, Communists, or Seventh-Day Adventists. I tried to appraise each person I worked with by what he stood for and what he did, not by what party he belonged to or what label had been slapped on him.

In the course of the activities I just outlined, I must have attended a hundred or so meetings; I don't recall that the name of Stalin was ever mentioned. The war was now over and his role in world affairs was no longer prominent. Nor did I ever hear of any secret encounters with Soviet agents on the corner of Hollywood and Vine in the dead of night. We had too many concerns of our own, and at the time the Russians were pretty busy rebuilding their devastated country. There may well have been an orthodoxy on the part of those among us who were party members—a "party line" it is called—to which they adhered as they did in the Washington hearings. But if so, it was their own, not Stalin's. I remember debates and arguments on questions, but no decisions were ever imposed on the rest of us in the progressive organizations to which we mutually belonged. Raising the issue of "Stalinism" in the context of blacklisted filmmakers seems to be something of a diversion from the political realities of that period.

Before appearing in Washington, those of us who had been served subpoenas gathered in Edward G. Robinson's home in Beverly Hills to discuss how to deal collectively with the situation confronting nineteen of us, the opening move in a campaign that was going to affect the entire film community and, eventually, the country at large. John Huston and Philip Dunne had organized what was termed the "Committee of a Hundred" to support us and defend our rights. Present at the meeting were many of Hollywood's celebrated figures, including Katharine Hepburn, Humphrey Bogart, Lauren Bacall, and John Garfield. After much discussion it was decided that as many of their committee as could get away would appear at the hearings on our behalf.

That nightmarish week in Washington will remain with me the rest of my life. We were in our own capital, yet no foreign city could have been more alien and hostile. All our hotel rooms were bugged. When we, the nineteen "unfriendly witnesses," wanted to talk with each other or with our attorneys, we had either to keep twirling a metal key to jam the circuit or to go out of doors. It became clear from the outset of the hearings that this was no impartial investigation or trial, but an inquisition, impure and simple, designed to break down, expose, and vilify the political and social beliefs of those who dissented from the now-established Cold War policies.

Although I was one of the nineteen, I was in one sense an outsider from my own group since I disagreed with the stand taken by the majority.

Led by members of what later became known as the "Hollywood Ten" and approved by all three of our lawyers, they decided not to answer any of the committee's questions relating to their political associations and beliefs. Their position was based on a literal interpretation of the First Amendment protecting an individual's freedom of belief and expression. I had every respect for their principled position and still have. My disagreement was purely tactical. I contended that in a period of public hysteria induced by the widely publicized "Red menace," the Bill of Rights would be disregarded or circumvented one way or another. My counterproposal was for all of us to speak out and defend affirmatively our own and each other's political beliefs and associations.

168 AS TIME GOES BY

Several of the ten and one of our lawyers tried hard to persuade me that theirs was the right course and that my stand would disrupt the unity of the "unfriendly nineteen." I argued that our refusal to answer would be interpreted by the press and the public as an admission of guilt, as proof of our having something to hide. Actually, there was nothing hidden from the committee. They knew who was and who wasn't a party member and, in fact, everything about us and our associations. For the past months they had planted informers to infiltrate and report on our activities. And any gap was filled in by the "friendly witnesses" who testified against us at the start of the hearings.

Since most of the ten and the lawyers were solidly against my proposal, I had misgivings: perhaps I was wrong, perhaps I was taking the easier way out since I was not a party member, although at that time there was no law making membership a crime. To test my position I met several times with John Huston at night on the street where our conversation couldn't be bugged. He listened to both sides of the argument, then talked it over with the Committee of a Hundred. He reported back to me that they agreed with my proposal and were willing to back it with full support of everyone under attack, whether a party member or not.

This failed to sway the ten, who confronted the Congressional committee with their refusals to answer, often eloquently. The First Amendment was brushed aside by the committee and later by the courts; the ten men eventually went to prison. Nine of the ten held steadfastly to their political beliefs and today, two decades later, receptions are held in their honor, books and plays are written, based on the transcripts of the hearings, in which they appear, deservedly, in the role of heroes.

One evening when it had become clear we were losing whatever public and industry support we once had, several of us were gathered in our hotel room talking over our plight. The mood was anything but cheerful. Paul Draper, the dancer and a long-time

friend, dropped in, took a look at us, and made a suggestion. Paul
stuttered in ordinary conversation but never on the stage.

"L-look, you guys. When you're as d-down as you are tonight,
there's only one th-thing to do."

We all turned and looked at him. What was he going to pro-
pose—suicide?

"You order the b-best champagne you can get and d-drink it
up. It never f-fails."

Anne thought it was a great idea; the rest of us went along.
Paul did the ordering. He knew the right vineyard and the best
vintage year, directing the wine steward to find what was wanted
even if he had to dig it out of the vaults. And it worked its bub-
bling magic. As the wine went down, our spirits rose. We became
almost euphoric, casting out all inhibitions. If the committee
played back on their recording machine what was said that night,
they must have heard some astonishing things.

This little spree was a much-needed antidote to what was going
on in the committee room. The "friendly witnesses" such as Jack
Warner, John Wayne, and Adolphe Menjou were cataloguing our
"political sins" in great detail and getting full coverage by the
press. Warner testified that in his opinion I was a "Communist";
the studio had had to get rid of me because I was "slipping Communist propaganda in their films." This had a special irony since
it was at his urgent request that I wrote the screenplay for *Mission to Moscow*, which had brought him kudos at the time but
was now obviously an embarrassment. I had no opportunity to
point this out at the hearings, as the committee canceled my
subpoena by a last-minute telegram, apparently not eager to have
me testify. Later Warner lamely admitted to a friend that he had
"made a mistake." However that might be, I am still listed in the
Congressional Record as Warner described me, which shows that
lies are preserved in these official volumes as carefully as the
truth.

The heads of the Hollywood studios, frightened by threats of boycotts of their films by the American Legion and like-minded groups, capitulated and began a wholesale purge of anyone suspected of Communist membership or leftist leanings.

Contracts were broken at will. The morals clause, equating nonconformity with immorality, provided a legal excuse. Caution dictated the pictures now being made. Any idea with the slightest social implication was taboo. Using the threat of boycott, the various committees and their adherents had captured a powerful communications medium which, for a time, had dared to question what had become official policy.

In social gatherings one had to be careful what subjects were discussed, and with whom. One even had to watch which movie houses one attended. (Avoid Russian films. Self-appointed spies could be lurking to record the identifying numbers on car license plates.) And this shadowed world had its physical counterpart. Smog had seeped in from the open storage tanks of the oil refineries and, fed by the increasing motor traffic, was casting its pall over Los Angeles and its environs.

In personal terms Anne and I survived the first onslaught of the blacklists. Our turn was to come later in a manner that had a comic as well as a serious side.

THE 13TH LETTER

In contrast to our growing disillusionment with Hollywood, Anne and I, despite our eastern origins, became enamorcd of the desert. We decided to move to Palm Springs, where we would have pure air to breathe, open country for horseback riding, and an eye feast of crinkly, elephant-hide mountains that changed color with every hour of the day. It was within easy reach of the studios; in fact, it was a sort of weekend extension of the movie colony.

The center of Hollywood gravitation in Palm Springs is the Racquet Club, that venerable institution on the north side of the town. Although I was not a habitué of the club, our desert life being so different from resort life that its only resemblance was geographical, I had various occasions to visit there, usually as a guest of a movie producer or director. The club, like most desert architecture, can best be described from inside out. At the center was the Kodachrome-blue swimming pool facing the glass-encased bamboo bar and dining room. Scattered over the several acres were tennis courts and cottages for the overnight guests—each a florist box of glass and pastel cement bowed and beribboned with flaming bougainvillea vines.

If I had a daytime appointment, it was usually to one of these cottages that I went, picking my way carefully around the shapely bodies of stars and starlets sitting by the pool tanning their valuable flesh under protective ointments. When I reached the producer's cottage I invariably found him in a dark living room, shuttered tightly against the sun, playing gin rummy with several of his moviemaking peers. Even though he had initiated the appointment with me, I could sense his reluctance to interrupt the game. It usually worked out that I watched for a while, pretending to be interested in the game as he later had to pretend to be interested in my ideas for the script.

Our conference, generally taking place in a shady part of the patio, was usually brief out of all proportion to the arrangements for it, like a miniature in an enormous frame. How many pages of the script had I done? Did I like it? Did my wife like it?—as though faith in a script, like charity, must begin at home. I struggled between modesty and honesty, knowing that any doubt I manifested he would quickly multiply by a thousand since the confidence a film executive feels in a literary property is, to put it mildly, variable.

The conference over, my host scurried back into the dark room and the interminable game. I often wondered why he came all the way to the desert to do the same thing he could do in his Hollywood office. The answer, I think, is the change that came over him and the club in the evening. When I was asked to a conference at the cocktail hour, I always enjoyed it more, not because we got more done, but because it took place in a more cheerful and receptive mood. As soon as the sun was safely bedded down behind Mt. San Jacinto, my hypothetical producer donned his white jacket and walked from his cottage to the bar (his exercise for the day), the social center of the club before dinner. Here, over a gin fizz or a rum punch, his mood was mellow, and if he hadn't lost too much at gin rummy during the day, every prospect pleased him. And why shouldn't it? Out of the large window he looked on the pool, dramatically lit, emerald and luminous against a darkening background. Around him were beautiful women, gorgeously gowned and displaying the tan they had worked all day to acquire. In such a gathering the listener heard more than mere talk, for "dialogue" was spoken. The lines, or lines like them, might have been said before—in a picture perhaps—but that was not important. They were delivered in a new context and with the skill to put them over. The timing was right; they made their point, got their laugh. And the spectator gradually became aware that what he was watching was not life being lived but a scene being played. Hollywood had found a place where its workaday world and its playtime world could merge. If the people in the industry are not always willing to make their pictures like life, I have found many of them eager to make their lives as much as possible like their pictures. This is what Palm Springs offered them—a dream world complete with a built-in mirage.

During this Shangri-la period, Otto Preminger, who years later was the first director to insist on crediting the blacklisted Dalton Trumbo for his work on *Exodus,* came down to Palm Springs to persuade me to do the screenplay for an English version of the French film entitled *The 13th Letter.* The material didn't exactly fascinate me and I had no liking for remakes. But Otto was an old friend from the stage; I accepted the assignment when he assured me that I could take liberties with the story, essentially a murder plot in which a middle-aged married couple were guilty participants, and that I could change the setting from France to Canada and add whatever ideas I thought would enhance its values.

A personal experience suggested an angle that would give their motivation for the crime a fresh twist. During my college days I had met a rotund young couple with whom I became friends. Freddie was an art teacher, talented and likable. Pudge was an artist, something of a pixie, whose paintings reflected her antic personality. After they left New York, I heard that Freddie had become head of the Art Department at Carnegie Tech. Then they dropped out of sight.

Years passed until one day they materialized out of nowhere, at my office in the writers' building at Warners. Freddie seemed little changed, but Pudge was pudgier and obviously harried. To my astonishment, she unveiled two black cats that had been concealed under the folds of her voluminous black cape. The last of their possessions, all they had in the world, was locked in their station wagon parked outside the studio gates.

Freddie was jobless and in need of money. As he was a knowledgeable and tasteful person, I was able to get him on the Warners payroll as technical adviser on *Three Strangers*, a picture I had written, based on a Huston story, starring Peter Lorre and Geraldine Fitzgerald.

With his sunny disposition, Freddie got along well with the director and cast, but Pudge began to create problems. She locked herself in Freddie's office while he worked on the set, emerging only when her husband reappeared at the end of the day. Her strange behavior caused talk and concern among the other occupants of the building, mostly writers and their secretaries. I realized I would have to do something. I went to their office and knocked. She opened the door a crack. When she saw who it was, I was allowed to enter. The room smelled of cats and stale food. She had also moved in the clothes and blankets that had been stored in their car. It looked as though they had been camping there, converting his office into a temporary home. Our conversation was not reassuring.

"Pudge, why do you stay locked in here? While Freddie's working, why don't you go out and enjoy yourself?"

Her eyes grew big. "Oh, no, we can't."

"Why not?"

"They're after us, that's why. They've been following us all across the country."

"They? Who's they?"

"Some people who don't like us." She turned away, stroking one of the cats. "They tried to poison us, didn't they, Precious?"

Precious purred and I blanched; I went down to the set and drew her husband aside. "Freddie, you've got to do something about Pudge." His reaction was one of surprise. "Why? What's the matter?"

"She's sick and she needs help."

Freddie gave me an incredulous look. "Why do you say she's sick?"

"She's got a crazy idea you and she and her cats are being chased, threatened by . . . I don't know who."

All the friendly warmth drained out of Freddie's face. He glared at me with open hostility, answering quietly, with deep conviction: "We are."

He turned and rejoined the others on the set. There was nothing I could do. In all other respects, Freddie's behavior was normal. He was doing his job well. But out of his devotion to his wife, he had apparently accommodated her paranoiac delusions until they had become as real to him as they were to her. It was a classic case of a rare malady—*folie à deux*.

After the production closed and Freddie's job was finished, the couple vanished without a good-bye, and that was the last I ever heard of them. But the incident remained vivid in my memory, and since all experiences are grist for a writer's mill, I determined to use it in my screenplay for *The 13th Letter* with Preminger's enthusiastic approval.

The film was to be made at the Fox studio, which was then under the aegis of Darryl Zanuck. When the first draft of my screenplay was submitted, Otto and I were called to the front office for a story conference. It was my first meeting with Zanuck; I had heard many tales of these conferences, but I didn't know quite what to expect. The office was impressive in its size, approximately the length of a bowling alley. Zanuck had read the script, and during the discussion he kept walking from his desk all the way to the far end of his office, almost out of sight, and entirely out of hearing. I felt we should have been equipped with a walkie-talkie to keep in contact. What finally emerged was that he liked the script, except for the revelatory *folie à deux* scene, which he said should be cut. Since this was the scene that I felt most necessary and original, I objected.

"But, Mr. Zanuck, this gives the basic motivation for the murder. Otherwise, the picture is just about any two psychopaths committing a crime."

"Well, that's what they are, aren't they?"

"Yes, but with a very special psychological problem connected with a man's love for his paranoiac wife. That's what makes it *folie à deux.*"

"The audience doesn't give a damn about *folie à deux.* They've come to see two crazy people committing murder."

"I don't agree. Without that particular relationship, the picture makes no real sense. It's an obligatory scene."

Zanuck, now finally in his chair and clearly visible, gave me a hard look. "In this studio, I decide what's obligatory."

That was it. The film was made without the *folie à deux.* From most of the critics it received better reviews than it deserved. From me, it got a bad notice. It was a body without a heart.

The political clouds were gathering and moving in our direction. Since the few assignments still being offered me were of little interest, I decided to initiate one of my own. I bought the movie rights to "Man in a Zoo," a short story by David Garnett, a prominent English author. It had very little in the way of incident but a unique central idea—a misanthropic man, at odds with his fiancée and the world in general, applies for admission to the London Zoo. He points out that the zoo has every animal on exhibit with the exception of *Homo sapiens,* in his mind a glaring omission. To the consternation of his fiancée but to the delight of the crowds that visit his cage, he quickly becomes the most popular attraction. Although much of the story remained to be written, it had obvious comic and satirical possibilities.

Since we had both been involved in various liberal causes, Charlie Chaplin and I had met on several occasions. Convinced that "Man in a Zoo" would be an ideal vehicle for his talents, I decided to try to interest him in working with me on the screen story and in playing the central role. I drove to his home in Beverly Hills, where we discussed the property's film potential. He became enthusiastic, and we agreed to work on it together.

By this time he was married to a handsome, somewhat reserved young woman, Oona O'Neill, the playwright's daughter, with whom he already had several children. They were devoted to each other and later made their home on their estate in Switzerland until his death. At the time of our collaboration they were planning a family trip abroad, and our work was interrupted.

Some time later, by chance, we were taking the same train across the country back to California. Charlie greeted me on the station platform with, "The old lady's pregnant again," referring to the youthful Oona. We arranged to meet in the club car at the cocktail hour to continue our discussions on "Man in a Zoo." At the start we made progress, but at subsequent meetings Charlie would come up with brand-new ideas, disregarding what we had already worked out. He would pantomime the action he was suggesting; the club car became crowded, the passengers getting a free performance by a master comedian. Soon I realized that Chaplin the actor was taking over from Chaplin my story collaborator. As much as I enjoyed our sessions, I saw that nothing final was going to eventuate, and the project never got off the ground.

RED ROSES
AND BLACK LISTS

According to the Old Testament, Adam and his female companion were cast out of Eden when she plucked the forbidden apple, and sex reared its fruitful head and all the begetting began. In our case, it was not an apple that banished us from our desert Eden but two dozen red roses.

When we moved out of Los Angeles, I handed in my resignation as chairman of the California Arts, Sciences and Professionals Council. The directors asked me to remain nominally as chairman until they could decide on a replacement, even though I would no longer be active. Anyway, by now the organization had lost whatever influence it once had. About all we did was send telegrams to Truman protesting this or that Cold War policy, which I feel certain were carefully filed in the presidential wastepaper basket.

In active charge of the ASP offices at that time was a very zealous executive secretary.

This was during the Korean War when American and South Korean forces, under MacArthur's command, were pressing the North Koreans back toward the border of China. The Chinese army was now massed at the border ready to join the North Koreans to halt the advance toward their territory. As a last-minute effort to avoid a confrontation, the Chinese sent a delegation to the United Nations in New York to discuss a possible peace initiative. In a well-intentioned but rather foolhardy gesture, the secretary sent two dozen red roses to the Chinese delegation, and she sent them in my name.

I knew nothing about it until the next morning when the *Los Angeles Times* had me splashed across the front page as a Benedict Arnold, giving aid and comfort to the enemy. For it was on that same day that, their mission fruitless, the Chinese entered the war and the two armies were shooting at each other.

John Wayne and other custodians of the blacklist were in full cry for my scalp. I had been on their "gray list" for a long time, and now they had an excuse (*cause célèbre*) to change the listing to black. The ASP directors, feeling responsible for my predicament, issued a statement that I had had nothing to do with the red roses incident, but explanations were useless.

Not because of sentiment, but because my pictures had made the studios a great deal of money, a powerful agent who shall be nameless asked me to come to his office; he had a proposition to make. He would arrange a meeting for me with the attorney who was the liaison to the House Un-American Activities Committee. All I had to do was spend a half-hour with this party, renouncing some of my unpopular political views and associates, and pay the attorney seventy-five hundred dollars. I told him that was a pretty expensive half-hour, both in money and in conscience.

He said, "Don't worry about the money. A studio will advance it as a down payment on a writing assignment."

"That isn't what I'm worried about. It's the other."

He brushed that concern aside. "What do you care what you tell those bastards? Keep your fingers crossed."

"I'd have to keep them crossed the rest of my life." I was curious. "Tell me, who gets the seventy-five hundred dollars? That's a pretty stiff fee for a half-hour of anyone's time."

"That's their business, not ours."

"Well, thanks for trying, but the answer is 'no.' "

"Don't decide now. This is your last chance to stay in pictures. Talk it over with your wife."

"Her answer wouldn't be any different."

He shook his head. "Too bad. You're throwing away a fine career."

I went back to Palm Springs. There was a black telephone in an alcove off the living room. I had never been conscious of how silent a phone could be until it stops ringing.

As living in Palm Springs was expensive and our savings limited, we sold our home and moved to Woodstock, New York, within easy distance from the surviving members of our two families. In Woodstock we found congenial friends and discovered that we could live comfortably on one-quarter of the money our California life-style had required.

In the meantime my New York agent was investigating my status on the "subversive lists" that were proliferating over the country far beyond the movie colony. Some were kept by official watchdog committees, others by private orgnizations such as Red Channels, and even by individuals such as the wholesale grocer in Syracuse who peddled names along with his canned goods. The lists being interchangeable, I was on most of them. Since the "Red" label could not be applied to nonparty persons, these custodians of the blacklists had to find other shadings such as "pinko" or "fellow traveler." Because of my friendships with some of the important movie names and my assumed influence on them, my agent found I was in a unique category. I was a "superdupe."

We have Superman, superstars, superathletes, supermarkets,

all highly regarded in our society, but I can't say I was enamored
of being labeled a dupe even with such an exalted prefix as *super*.
Anyway, the agent's conclusion was that unless I was willing to
admit the error of my ways, which I wasn't, there was little chance
of employment in Hollywood for the foreseeable future. We began to wonder what would happen when our savings ran out.
This we never had to face, as our problem was solved for us in
an unexpected way.

EXILE

Rome and Paris

I could hardly think of a more unlikely source for renewing our writing careers than a former Rumanian promoter. Since his film-making credentials were as dubious as the royalty claim of the famous Beverly Hills restaurateur, I shall call him Mr. Roman without the *off*.

As Lillian Hellman pointed out in her book *Scoundrel Time*, the blacklists were a boon to promoters of this type, as they could acquire established writers for their projects at cut-rate prices. Mr. Roman had read an original screen treatment of mine called *An Ordinary Spring*, which belied its title, ushering in one of the most extraordinary springs in our lives. Mr. Roman sought us out in Woodstock, locating us through my agent. He was the right casting for his role—agreeable, smooth-talking, carefully groomed, well mannered in the European tradition. He proposed that we come to Europe at his expense, where I would complete the screenplay based on my treatment and then work with translators, since he planned to produce the picture in three languages for worldwide distribution.

Having no better alternative, we gladly accepted his offer, but neither Anne nor I really believed the European trip would materialize. Becoming the writer-guests in a foreign country of a man we scarcely knew had an element of fantasy. In fact, we had almost put it out of our minds when a letter suddenly appeared with documents of prepaid passage to Naples on the S.S. *Independence* for the two of us and Peter, our five-year-old son. The sailing date was the following week. It was real after all, at least up to this point. As to the future, we would have to put our trust in the gods and our self-appointed "godfather." So began my Life Number Three, if anyone is still counting.

When we boarded the *Independence* for our first ocean voyage, we found we were traveling first-class, even with petty cash waiting for us in the purser's care. So far, Mr. Roman was doing well by us.

The bay of Naples, blue water and colored sails; the city with its narrow twisting streets and its vociferous inhabitants, very foreign to American eyes and ears. Having taken six years of Latin in high school and college, I had a naive hope that Italian would come easily to me. Anne eventually acquired a tourist vocabulary, but I never got much beyond *"Quanto costa?"* Escorted by a voluble guide, we were whisked through customs. Italian officials were not worried about spies or "subversives" entering their country. They left this concern to the American embassy, then headed by the watchful Clare Boothe Luce. It was rumored that our overstaffed embassy was so stocked with political dossiers on both natives and foreigners that whenever the Italian police wanted information on any of their own citizens, they went, not to their own Intelligence Bureau, but to the American source at the embassy.

With much handshaking, our guide saw us off at the train for

Rome, where it had been arranged that we stay at the elegant Hotel Hassler on a rise above the Spanish Steps. Our "godfather" was still providing only the best. By this time we were so entranced by the beauty and strangeness of our surroundings that we began to regard the blacklist as a passport to an experience we might otherwise have missed.

That evening Mr. Roman and his handsome young wife called for us at the hotel and took us to dinner at Alfredo's—where else? By this time we were becoming so spoiled that a second-class restaurant would have shocked our sensibilities. Up to now I had harbored some doubts about our benefactor, but in this setting, seduced by the finest vintage wines, I was ready to regard him as an out-of-season Santa Claus. For the finishing touch, Alfredo, or perhaps his manager (I was by this time in an alcoholic haze), came to our table and presented Anne with a gold spoon, awarded each evening to the one chosen as the most attractive female guest. However, the restaurant thriftily reclaimed the spoon at the end of the meal.

The Latin commentaries—Caesar, Cicero, and Terence—that I had so laboriously read came to life in the next few days as we explored the ancient city. On these wanderings I asked myself if life in ancient Rome was so different from that of our own times. In degree, yes. The Roman emperors had their spies and informers, as we do, but when a dissenter was fingered as a possible enemy during the reign of Tiberius, for instance, the emperor didn't bother with court procedures; he simply had his slaves push the suspect off the high cliff in front of his villa on Capri. The Forum was the scene of much jingoistic oratory—"Carthage must be destroyed"—and at least one notable assassination. We have the same kind of congressional oratory—"the Soviet Union must be out-missiled"—but in assassinations of public figures I'm not sure but what we are not ahead of the Romans.

One of the joys of our Roman holiday was that we never had to think of money. For our day-to-day expenses our host would hand us a wad of whatever currency was used in the particular country. In Italy, of course, it was liras. He was careful never to give us a check so that his name didn't appear with that of a blacklisted writer. But that didn't matter to us. I simply stuffed the bills in my pocket or in Anne's purse. Whenever it ran out, I would let him know and another wad was supplied. It was like make-believe money children invent for their games, but it served the very real purpose of taking care of all our needs and our pleasures.

Money can mean so many different things to different people. For some it buys power and influence, for others display; or it can provide a measure of security. I have never been rich, nor have I been really poor. There have been times when I was low in cash or in debt, but always there would turn up some way of earning money to get along, and in my Hollywood years there was too much to spend, often foolishly. But the beauty of having money to me is not having to think of money. And with our "godfather" footing all our bills, I was never more free from having to consider what we could or could not afford. During this strange interim period we could do whatever at the moment appealed to us.

However, I am afflicted with a conscience that at times awakens and intrudes on my hedonism. After a week of eating, drinking, and sight-seeing, I asked Mr. Roman, "When do I start on the script?"

"When you get to Paris." He had it all planned. "I've rented an apartment there where you can do the screenplay. How long will it take?"

"About six weeks."

"Good. But first you and I are going location hunting in Austria. I've got plane tickets for tomorrow."

"What about Anne and Peter?"

"That's all arranged. They'll be in Paris when you get back."

This was the pattern of the next several months. Go here, go there—we never knew when or for how long. All decisions were made for us.

My screen story was based partly on a friend's actual experience during the liberation of her German village from the Nazis by American troops. During the occupation, she fell in love with an American soldier and in her brief idyllic affair she experienced the first "ordinary spring" in her war-ravaged girlhood. For financial reasons Mr. Roman wanted the town's locale moved to Austria, which made no difference as far as the essential romance and lyrical mood were concerned.

From Salzburg, we explored the surrounding countryside. The isolated, picture-postcard villages in the Austrian Alps had changed little from the Middle Ages. I suppose *quaint* is the definitive word, in both costume and architecture. For our film, Roman and I settled on one that seemed the most photogenic, providing the most contrast to the mechanical interventions that war brings in its wake.

The decision made, our producer-host returned to Rome while I went to Paris, where Anne and Peter were already established in living quarters so Parisian in furnishings and ambience that they could have existed nowhere else. It was on the top floor of a three-story building, each apartment facing a central courtyard. Two blocks away was the Eiffel Tower and a short distance farther the Seine. To Anne and me it all added up to the ultimate in Frenchness. Peter, spending half-days in a French preschool group, was at first not quite so entranced, but he enjoyed the sight-seeing and especially the French restaurants where we went for our evening meals: he developed an addiction to snails cooked the French way with much garlic. Our favorite restaurant was a family bistro, La Grille, in the Les Halles section, where we learned to prefer their wines, red and white, to our customary martinis. Even Peter acquired a taste for Beaujolais, although we watered it heavily, to the waiter's disapproval. It seems French children start drinking wine with their mother's milk.

Returning one night a little later than usual, we found that the massive doors that opened into the courtyard from the street were locked and we had only our apartment key. We had to phone an American friend, another exiled writer, who called the concierge, who, with much grumbling, let us in. When we asked him for a key, he said he was told by the landlord not to give us one. This was our first hint that we were not entirely welcome as tenants. From the maid we learned some strange things about our landlord, or rather Mr. Roman's landlord, since we were only temporary occupants. It seems that the owner was a hero of the French Resistance, in fact so famous for his exploits during the German occupation that a neighboring street was named for him. He lived in a top-floor apartment on the opposite side of the courtyard with an Englishman, also a former Resistance fighter, while his wife occupied rooms on the ground floor. They had two sons, handsome boys about ten and twelve. Although I played ball with them and Peter in the courtyard, I never knew where they lived or with which parent, since they didn't speak English. And when I tried to talk to them in fractured French, they would go off into gales of laughter. After a while we became friends with the boys, but their father didn't look us up nor did he revoke the order to withhold the key to the outer gate.

When he had the door to the small furnace that heated our apartment removed so that the fire kept going out—and it was a cold spring in Paris—we knew that the persecution was deliberate. Obviously it was his way of saying he didn't want us there regardless of Mr. Roman's lease on the apartment.

If he really thought he could get rid of us by this kind of sabotage, he reckoned without Anne. An engineer's daughter, she had the resources to cope with mechanical problems—and most other kinds, as I've discovered over the years. She took a silver tray from our apartment and managed to wedge it in the place where the furnace door had been taken off, and the fire recovered its bloom. To solve the front entrance barricade, she gathered pebbles and stuffed them in the keyhole so that the doors couldn't be locked. The concierge, cursing, wrestled with the problem to no avail. He would have had to take down the massive doors to empty the pebbles, and this task he was unwilling to undertake. From then on, we came and went as we pleased.

Since Paris architecture is fairly consistent, one of the city's many virtues, certain sections looked alike, at least to our eyes, so that sometimes we were lost. I remember one night we had dinner at a restaurant in an unfamiliar part of the city. After the meal, we started walking toward home—taxis were scarce at night except on the boulevards. Soon we hadn't the slightest idea whether we were walking toward our apartment or away from it. It was past Peter's bedtime, and he was getting cranky, which didn't help matters.

There were few passersby at this late hour and on this street. Finally, we caught sight of a young Frenchman, and overtaking him, we asked him, "*s'il vous plaît*," to help us out. He spoke no English and our French was inadequate. To give him some idea of where we lived, I kept repeating "*La Seine*" but in my Americanized pronunciation it came out *sane*, so the puzzled Frenchman only shook his head. Again, it was Anne who solved the dilemma. Her ability to reproduce sounds is a steady source of amusement on two continents and has a long history. Before CBS radio stations devised their modern sound equipment, Anne, then the eighteen-year-old secretary of one of the department heads in the New York office, would be called down to the studio to produce whatever sound effect they lacked and needed for a particular program. Years later I was told by an actor who was on the show that on one occasion she clucked out a sound that must have been the high point in her avocation—the clatter of horse's hooves on cobbled pavement, *backing up*. I might not have believed this if I wasn't a long-time witness to her vocal accomplishments: snatches of popular songs (usually relevant to something that was happening); the tremolo of an opera singer (burlesque); a whole aviary of bird whistles; the trickle of a leaky pipe (this to inform a plumber); an ailing spark plug in our car motor (this for the garage mechanic). Among our friends she is known affectionately as "noisy Anne," but this is not quite fair because she also puts a high value on silence.

On this particular occasion I was confident Anne would find some way to communicate our problem to the person we'd encountered. Before the stranger's astonished eyes her fingers rippled like small waves and soon I heard the splashing of water against a riverbank, punctuated by the low, mournful toots of a French riverboat. At first our friend looked completely bewildered, then suddenly his face lit up with a happy smile.

"*Ah, la Seine!*"

He pointed in the right direction, and once we reached the river, the rest was easy. The pebbles were still doing their work and soon we were safely in our apartment. The overtired Peter made one testy comment, addressed to the French public in general: "I don't see why they can't speak English."

Meanwhile I worked every morning and within the six-week period had a first-draft screenplay. The story was simple, depending for its interest on the nuances in the development of the love affair between the two young people from such vastly different backgrounds.

Then one day the phone rang and through the vocal maze of French and Italian operators I heard the voice of our producer, calling from Rome. He now wanted us in a German town named Gruenwald, outside Munich, where an ex-Hollywood refugee writer would work with me on a German translation of my screenplay; I was also to mail him a copy in Rome. As usual, no time was lost. We were to leave that night on the Orient Express bound for Munich. An assistant of Mr. Roman's would be at the train with tickets for the journey.

We packed hastily, called our good-byes to a few American expatriate friends, and informed the concierge of our departure. Then the unexpected happened: our elusive French landlord

and his English roommate appeared at our door. They were in
their thirties, of pleasing appearance with nothing in their manner to suggest the homosexual, bisexual, or whatever. We invited
them in, supposing they wanted to inspect the condition of the
apartment. Apparently a quick glance reassured them.

They were polite if somewhat restrained. We felt we were
under scrutiny, but we didn't know quite why since we were on
the point of leaving their premises. Anne invited them to sit
down and offered to make them tea, which to our surprise they
accepted._It was evident the Frenchman had something on his
mind, and suddenly he opened up the subject in English with
only a slight trace of accent.

"If you will excuse me, what are you doing here?"

"Working on a screenplay for a movie."

"But why here? You are Americans."

"It's a long story." I was not sure I should go into it, but they
looked genuinely interested. "Well, you see, we have some political problems back home—the McCarthy business. They don't
like our views—left-wing they call them, or sometimes even
Communist—so we've been blacklisted. Do you know what
'blacklisted' means?"

Our landlord exchanged glances with his friend, then looked
back at us. His expression softened. "Yes, we know very well
what that means." He gave us a slight smile. "We have political
troubles here too, we who were in the Resistance."

It was my turn to be surprised. "But how can that be? We
heard that you were a hero in the movement."

"We only did what many others did. But you can be a hero
one year and a suspect the next, even watched by the police. *You*
must understand that."

I nodded. "Have things changed that much in France?"

Some of the bitterness he felt crept into his voice. "Your
Marshall Plan—"

I interrupted. "Not *our* Marshall Plan."

"I understand that. But your government has seen to it—with

money—that all the wrong people, from our point of view, the Resistance point of view, are now in power in our country."

"So we're more or less in the same boat. I'm sorry."

The Frenchman shook his head. "It is we who should be sorry —sorry for what we did to you and Madame—"

"Anne." She supplied the missing word while pouring the tea. Our landlord looked at her with a smile. It usually takes the French about a year's acquaintance before they feel familiar enough to use first names. On this occasion, our landlord was so intrigued he repeated the name as though tasting it and finding it good.

"Anne. And my name is Pierre, and this is Derek," referring to his companion.

Suddenly we were all laughing and on a first-name basis, which they seemed to enjoy as though taking part in some new tribal custom. Pierre, still feeling guilty about the attempts at sabotage, went on to explain. "Not only the politics, but we were not always happy with . . . some Americans we have met here."

The hesitation told us he was referring to Mr. Roman without wishing to name him. "And now you are going away." He shook his head. "If only we had known . . ."

We assured him that no explanation was necessary.

"And now, Anne, if you will permit, we will finish your tea with some wine to celebrate the occasion."

He left and quickly reappeared with a bottle of champagne, and we drank to better times in both our countries. In any kind of encounter we found the French to be compulsive handshakers and by now we had become so friendly that when they left, we must have shaken hands all around about fifteen times, Peter included. Thinking it must be some sort of French game, he entered with great gusto.

The Orient Express left at midnight. Taking all our luggage, we spent our last evening at La Grille. Knowing from experience that Peter is not at his best late at night, we watered his wine a little less and I remember that, by train time, three homeless, slightly groggy Americans were in such high spirits that we neither knew nor cared what we would find at the end of our journey. By now it all blended into just another episode in what had become, not real life anymore, but a continuing adventure.

Germany

Agatha Christie, wherever you are, you're a good mystery writer and we forgive you, but I hope no one writes any more romantic stories about the Orient Express. At least not about the rather shabby train we boarded that night in May of 1952. Not a single murder occurred, not even a robbery or an authenticated rape. Where were the Russian secret police and our own CIA? Why weren't they skulking down the aisles, tailing each other as respectable spies are supposed to be doing? Didn't they know there was a Cold War on? Perhaps they were too busy spying on their own people. Anyway the whole experience was quite a letdown from our high expectations.

At the French border we were awakened by peremptory knocks on the door of our compartment. Still hazy from our evening's wine fest, I fumbled my way to the door and opened to two surly French customs officials who demanded to see our passports. By this time passports were a sensitive subject with American political refugees, since word had spread that the State Department was revoking them whenever they could locate their holders. I held them out for the officials to inspect without handing them over. They made no effort to take them, just asked the usual questions—where are you going and why? As if it made any difference in world affairs. I answered them, they grunted an assent, and I lurched my way back to my couchette.

Again I had just fallen asleep when the same heavy raps on the door woke me up. This time it was two German customs officials with the same questions. By this time I was convinced that the people of all countries could get along much better if all officials were removed from their jobs and put to honest labor. If that made me an anarchist, so be it—but a very sleepy one.

Our stay in Munich was brief and our remembrances few but vivid. We enjoyed German beer, served out of kegs. And we learned to like venison, well aged and delicious. We visited the beer hall where Hitler held forth during his rise to power (no thanks for the memory). But what impressed us most was the incredible energy of the people, from the *hausfrauen* scrubbing the sidewalks in front of their homes to the workers rebuilding the bombed-out city. Phoenix-like, Munich seemed to be rising out of its ashes right before our eyes. There were few cars, but bicyclists, knapsacks strapped to their shoulders, looking straight in the direction they were going, swarmed over the cobbled streets. The crowning touch was a huge sign high on the ruins of one of their factories: "SEND CARE PACKAGES TO BRITAIN." Only seven years had passed since their defeat and the vanquished people were being asked to give material aid to one of the victors. Was the sign an intended German mockery or, since it was spelled out in English letters, was it the work of a British occupation soldier, making a real plea to get help for his country? Whichever it was, what more graphic symbol could there be of a reversal of fortunes, with the victor impoverished by the war he had won?

Gruenwald was a small village on the Isar River twenty kilometers from Munich. Following Mr. Roman's instructions, we settled in the town's only hotel, called a *schloss*, having once been a castle. No one in the place spoke a word of English, and our German vocabulary was limited to *ja, nein, bitte* (please), *haferflocken* (oatmeal), and *schnapps*, hardly enough to familiarize ourselves with local convenience and customs. And so far our translator friend had not put in an appearance.

One custom we innocently violated caused a minor incident in the hotel. Our rooms were furnished with a toilet and washbasin, but the bathroom was a few doors away and was kept locked so that shaving was difficult and a bath impossible. We protested to the maid on our floor, but we couldn't understand what she said; the garbled exchange produced no key. As in Paris, Anne accepted this as a challenge to her ingenuity. One morning when the maid left the bathroom door open while she went to replace the towels, Anne saw her opportunity. She appropriated the key, and from then on the bathroom was at our disposal.

But consternation reigned throughout the *schloss*. Evidently this was a cardinal sin we had committed, but how to communicate that to some crazy Americans who had paid for their rooms and couldn't be ejected? However, this was their problem, not ours. The manager, a nervous, woebegone man in his fifties, pleaded with us every time we passed his desk, *"Bitte—der schlüssel."* By now we gathered that *schlüssel* was the key but we had no intention of giving it up, so we just shook our heads and made a helpless gesture of not understanding him. When we went out, the *schlüssel* safely in Anne's bag, we left the poor man on the verge of tears.

The dilemma was resolved with the arrival of Heinz Herald, a small, cheerful man who had the distinction of having been

thrown out of two countries, first Hitler's Germany, then Mc-
Carthy's America. We knew Heinz from our Hollywood days
and were delighted that Mr. Roman had picked him to translate
my script into German. When we told him about the stolen key,
he laughed, explaining that a guest in a Bavarian hotel was required by custom to pay the maid for each use of the bathroom
a trivial amount, whereupon she opens the door and runs the
bath. Anne returned the *schlüssel* to the manager, who showered
dankeshöns on her in his heartfelt thankfulness. Order had returned to the *schloss*.

But not for long. We managed to create another crisis, and
this time Peter was the culprit. Since there were no English-
speaking schools in Gruenwald, American children, mostly of
parents connected with the occupation forces, were picked up
each morning by an army truck and taken to an improvised classroom. Peter, the youngest boy in the crowded vehicle, looked
pretty forlorn as he rode off from the *schloss* with a truckload of
strangers more accustomed to living in a foreign country.

Afternoons, as a compensation, Peter was given his choice of
recreations. Unfortunately, he settled on one that, to say the
least, was unique—snail hunting. While Heinz Herald and I
worked on the translation, Anne would take him down to the
banks of the Isar River, which, from our experience, must be the
home of more snails than any other body of water in the world.
This could have been a harmless sport if it had ended there.
But after making his daily catch, Peter would insist on bringing
them back to the *schloss*.

Before long our rooms were crawling with snails—on the floor,
in our beds, in the clothes closet. At night we'd be awakened by
the creatures dragging their slimy bodies over our faces.

Our cleaning maid reported the invasion to the manager, and
again the *schloss* was in a state of confusion. How to get rid of
the snails without losing their paying guests? Finally, the maid
put an end to the affair when one of the more adventurous
mollusks crawled up her leg. She let out a shriek and turned on

us in a rage. *"Nein! Nein! Nein Schneckenhausen,"* pointing to the offending creatures. From *schloss* to *schlüssel* to *schneckenhausen*—at least we were progressing in our German. Reluctantly Peter collected the *"schneckenhausen"* from various parts of our room and took them back to the Isar, where, for all I know, their progeny are prospering and multiplying to this day.

Through Heinz Herald we found an elegant German restaurant within walking distance of the hotel. The food, the wine, the ambience were so to our liking that we spent all our evenings there. Occasionally we were joined by Heinz or Wolfgang Rheinhardt, who was temporarily staying in the area. Whatever uncertainties we felt about the future—and they were beginning to seep in—were washed down by our favorite Rhine wine. And since snails were on the menu, Peter was by now reconciled to the loss of his precious *"schneckenhausen."*

One of the added attractions was the indigenous background music of a zither, soft, dulcet, almost the whisper of a song. This was the time when the "Third Man Theme" was being played everywhere, and the zither peculiarly suited that haunting tune. Each evening it was a request number on the program.

After we had become regular patrons of the restaurant, the musician asked if we had any song we'd like to hear. Before leaving Hollywood a composer friend, Earl Robinson, had written a charming theme song for *An Ordinary Spring.* We had no sheet music of the song but we knew the words, "I just want an ordinary spring . . ." and so on, and Anne (the sound specialist) could hum the tune, which the zither player quickly learned by ear. After that, each evening when we entered the restaurant the musician greeted us with a few bars of "An Ordinary Spring." Since the tune soon vied in popularity with the "Third Man Theme," we began to build some extravagant hopes that our eventual film might do the same.

But by now the calls and letters had stopped coming from Mr. Roman and our supply of marks was running dangerously low. We called the hotel in Rome and the apartment in Paris.

No Mr. Roman anywhere. He had disappeared to wherever promoters hole up when they don't want to be reached. Much later we learned that the financing of the film project had collapsed. Instead of telling us, he found it easier to abandon us.

Anne and I held a council. We could try to locate Mr. Roman in Italy or France, but that seemed hopeless. I had heard that a Swiss producer had been trying to reach me to discuss a screenplay assignment, but this was rather vague and chancy. Having no desire to return to America, still under the McCarthy cloud, we settled on London, where we had friends, fellow exiles, and where we might get film work from English companies.

Peter, who had been listening to these new plans, looked troubled. In twelve months he had attended schools on both coasts of the United States and in three foreign countries—not exactly an ideal program for a five-year-old. The *schneckenhausen* notwithstanding, he had done pretty well. But now he looked up at us with a wistful expression. "London? What language do they speak there?"

London

One advantage of being a member of a minority is the close ties with others in the same racial, religious, or other grouping—in our case, political refugees drawn together by our common predicament. Fragments of Hollywood were scattered over the Western world, seeding new movie colonies in Rome, Paris, London, and Mexico. If you belonged, you soon knew every other exiled American in whatever place you settled. Each new arrival could count on assistance from those already established. The mutual aim was survival, if possible in our own field; if not, in whatever way a living could be earned.

On our arrival at the London airport, we were met by Phil and Ginny Brown, an American couple who had put down early roots in English soil, or, more accurately, in English water, as they were living in a houseboat on the Thames west of London.

They had purchased an old barge, and Ginny being a skilled craftsperson (in America she had made custom footwear), they had fixed up the boat into a comfortable and attractive home which they aptly named *Mayflower II*, being latter-day pilgrims in reverse.

The Browns had already rented a flat for us in South Kensington, and we moved right in without having to spend money on a hotel room. That evening during dinner on the houseboat, they filled us in with useful information on everything from where to shop to where to look for writing assignments. An actor-director, Phil was by now familiar with the English theatrical and movie worlds. The first step, he advised, was to find a strong agency to represent us.

"But do they want Americans? There are good English writers."

"In films they prefer Americans. I suppose because Hollywood movies play everywhere and make the most money."

"How about the blacklist? Doesn't that make us suspect?"

"The English, at least those we've met, despise McCarthyism."

I was still not convinced. "McCarthy is only the visible symbol of repression. They're in the Cold War with us, aren't they?"

"Their government is, but the English people like Americans. They think of McCarthyism as a disease that we'll get over."

"So it can't happen here?"

"I don't think so. Here you can think and say what you like." Phil grinned. "Just don't slander the queen."

I thought of our recent experience in Munich. "It's funny—in Germany I wasn't sure who won the war. They seem in better shape than our allies. Now I'm not even certain who won the revolution."

Phil laughed. "Forget politics. Go get a movie job. With your credits, it should be a cinch."

Phil was right. The next day I was signed by a prestigious agency, Christopher Mann, located at Marble Arch, the gateway to the London theatrical world. And within a month I had a contract with Rank, the leading British movie production company, to write the screenplay for a major film. It was to star Elizabeth Taylor, on loan from United Artists, which had agreed to distribute the picture in America. The fee was much lower than my established price in Hollywood, but one could live well in London on much less. That night we celebrated with dinner at Wheeler's in Soho, famous for its seafood, then a show in a West End theatre.

Our euphoria was short-lived. A week later Rank asked my agent if I would cancel our contract. He explained that when United Artists learned I was to write the screenplay, they informed Rank that they could not distribute the picture in the United States with my name on it. The blacklist had a long arm! Although legally I could have held Rank to the contract, I agreed to cancel since it was no fault of theirs and they needed American distribution to justify the cost of the production.

At that point Anne and I were rechristened. She became "Anne Rodney," and I, "Peter Howard." It was that simple. We didn't need an edict from the Church of England or an Act of Parliament. With my new identity I wrote the screenplays for several independent producers, but my most ambitious project had a stormy history.

I wrote a science fiction story and screenplay titled *The Island* about a Howard Hughes–type character who flies his experimental plane at such velocity that he loses his bearings in space. He lands on what appears to be an island whose inhabitants live by a set of values in marked contrast to those of the competitive world he left. At first, he resists what he considers their primitivism, but through his relationship with a girl and her father who rescued him, he begins to accept their cooperative way of life. Then he is told the secret they have withheld from him: the "island"—the future—and the island people are the survivors of a nuclear holocaust, living in a future dimension. In the end, he is permitted to reconstruct his plane and fly back into the present. My story leaves the question open—is the future preordained, or can man change its course and avert the disaster my protagonist had either experienced or envisioned?

For my technical adviser, I was fortunate to have Arthur Clarke, the head of the British Astrophysical Society, and later the celebrated author of *Childhood's End* and *2001*. Although my story moved into imaginary realms, it rested on a premise postulated by Einstein, called the Time Retardation Theory, for which Arthur supplied the scientific information.

Jack Hawkins, then the top English box-office star, liked the story and agreed to play the lead. The production was set up under the auspices of Columbia-British, which was willing to distribute a film written by Howard Koch so long as Peter Howard took the credit.

Then came the blow. On a trip to Spain seeking outdoor shooting locations, the producer, Edana Romney, and the director, Peter Glenville, both strong-minded, had a serious falling out. On his return Glenville called me. I tried to persuade him not to let what happened affect his commitment to the picture, but it was no use. He resigned, and since Jack Hawkins wanted him, we lost our star and with him the money, the production, a year's work, and all the hopes of putting a story on the screen that had serious social implications long before the nuclear arms buildup that threatens us today.

Anne had better luck. She wrote some of the original "Robin Hood" television scripts, starring Richard Green, for Hannah Weinstein, an expatriate who had raised enough money from English sources to launch the series.

Having gained the confidence of some London financial backers, Hannah was soon in a position to provide employment for a number of blacklisted writers living in England. The benefits were mutual. The "Robin Hood" series was so successful worldwide that she became wealthy and purchased a manor house outside London where she was a generous host to stranded Americans.

During this stage of our exile, working at whatever came our way, we had few complaints and no regrets over the choices we had made, or that had been made for us. Peter liked the English schools. Our home was a large, handsomely furnished house on Phillimore Gardens, backing on Holland Park with its cricket fields within view, and with the historical reminder that Lord Byron strolled through these same flowered paths with his reputed mistress, Lady Holland. The house came equipped with a maid and a handyman. In addition, we acquired a lovely Spanish au pair girl who lived with us as part of the family, doing much of the cooking, freeing Anne for her script work.

Among our neighbors in Holland Park was Carl Foreman, another blacklisted writer with screenplay credits on several noteworthy American films in his background. An ambitious and talented man, he became a writer-producer, associated with such films as *Bridge over the River Kwai,* and in later years became president of the English Screenwriters Guild. From a "man without a country" status in the McCarthy era, Carl climbed into prominence in the film circles of two countries.

We had a closer association with Joseph Losey. In Hollywood we had known Joe and his then wife (it seems most wives of our movie friends become "then"). Since our house in Phillimore Gardens was larger than we needed, we sublet the top floor to Joe, who became half tenant and half houseguest.

Actually, for a blacklisted person, his career was not going badly. He directed a few small-budget pictures, one of which I wrote for an independent company. The film was of no importance, but it played all over England and even made its way to America. Later Joe formed an association with Harold Pinter, who wrote the screenplay for one of his most successful pictures, *The Servant.*

Observing Losey's work over the years, I appreciated his sensitivity to character values, but I feel something is lacking. For want of a more precise word, I would call it fidelity—seeing an idea all the way through to its logical end. Individual scenes are beautifully handled, but too often the story line seemed to

swerve at some crucial point, losing its way to a satisfying conclusion. Perhaps I do him an injustice. If so, I do it with respect
for his talents and for his political convictions, for which he
would make no compromises.

Within a year we felt very much at home in London. Light
rain and fog were fairly constant, but this seemed somehow appropriate to the silver ambience of the city. History was written
in blue plaques on the walls of buildings. In our country, often
we tear down the old in favor of something new and usually
bigger, but the English treasure and preserve their past—the
birthplaces and haunts of their famous writers, statesmen, and
national heroes. Anne and I had martinis in the pub where
Charles Lamb and Coleridge drank their gin and bitters over
conversation that has become part of our literary heritage. Since
I had begun a play on the Lambs and their bohemian circle, this
was of particular interest. Renting a car, we explored the Shake-
speare country and parts of Scotland. Except for attending one
peace meeting in Trafalgar Square, addressed by Bertrand
Russell, we lived very private lives and forgot about politics and
governments. But, unhappily, our government did not forget us.

Anne and I were summoned to the embassy by a letter from
the American consul. On our way into his offices, we noticed a
statue of Franklin Roosevelt on the grounds fronting the embassy. Somehow heartened by this friendly reminder, we went
into the meeting with the consul, a gray-haired man with a
pleasant smile, not at all the officious bureaucrat our imaginations had conjured up. After a polite exchange he came to the
point, obviously with reluctance.

"I'm sorry, but I have to ask you to turn over your passports."

My reply was not reluctant: "I'm sorry, too, but we have to
refuse. We got the passports legally, paid for them. They're
ours."

"Only by consent of the State Department, and they've re-
quested you return them."

"On what grounds?"

"I can't go into that."

Anne had listened, saying nothing. Now she asked a question. "The man whose statue you have outside the embassy—did they take away *his* passport?"

The consul gave her a puzzled look. "I don't think I see the connection."

Evidently Anne felt no need to elaborate, so I filled in the gap. "What my wife means is that what we've done politically was in line with what President Roosevelt stood for. So there seems to be a certain inconsistency in erecting a statue to him and taking away our passports."

The consul glanced down at the paper on his desk, which we surmised was a list sent him of our "misdeeds."

"You wrote *Mission to Moscow.*"

This was a clincher. Smiling, I pointed toward the statue. "Yes, at his request. I mean the film was made at his request."

The consul changed to a more paternal approach. "Even if you hold your passports, they can be canceled. That means you can't travel anywhere except to the United States. Wouldn't it be better for you to go back to your own country and work things out there?"

I shook my head. "Go back where we're not wanted? Where they won't even let us work? . . . No, we'll stay here where our rights are respected."

The consul was silent for several moments and then evidently decided to trust us. His tone became warm. "Look, I don't particularly enjoy this part of my job, but I'm acting under orders. I hope you understand that." He rose. "I'll see what I can do."

We shook hands and thanked him. We never heard another word about our passports. They remained in force. Perhaps the consul was a holdover from the State Department in the Roosevelt administration, and luckily for us, his sympathies were still rooted in that more libertarian era.

Socially, the Americans had two focal points, one centering around Hannah Weinstein in Knightsbridge, the other around

Ella and Donald Ogden Stewart, who owned Frognal, once the Ramsey MacDonald home in Hampstead. Ella was a long time political figure, having been previously married to the great muckraker for liberal causes—Lincoln Steffens. Her hobby was art collecting. On the walls of their house hung paintings of the leading French Impressionists; Ella had purchased the paintings before the artists were world-famous. Now, when money was needed to maintain their standard of living, a painting would be sold, reluctantly but profitably. Now blacklisted, Donald had been a successful playwright-screenwriter in America, and a member of the literary coterie that included Dorothy Parker, Heywood Broun, Alexander Woollcott, and other celebrities of the Algonquin tradition. Each Sunday afternoon they held open house for their friends, American and English, who had standing invitations. Anne and I were among the "regulars." It was an occasion for reunions with old friends and meeting new people, either living in London or passing through on the way to Paris, Rome, New York, or wherever.

Ingrid Bergman was there one Sunday on her return from Casablanca. She told me she had gone there to see how close it was to the way we had portrayed it in the film. Some of the exterior scenes bore a resemblance, but, of course, there was no café like Rick's, no personality like Bogart's. At the time *Casablanca* was made, and even after it opened, Ingrid had reservations about the picture. Now that the film had become a popular classic, she was impressed enough to journey to its geographical namesake.

Embittered by the hostile treatment he had received in America for his political views and associations, Charlie Chaplin and his wife, Oona, had left the United States to settle in Vevey, Switzerland. On their frequent trips to London, they were guests at the Stewarts'. It was my first meeting with Charlie since our abortive film project. He was in fine form. Having recently visited Japan, he entertained the gathering one Sunday with a graphic account of his adventures there. I still remember his description of his first bath given by a female attendant. Fully clothed and with no props, Charlie pantomimed his embarrassed nakedness, at the same time suggesting his sexual titillation under the professional ministrations of the Japanese girl. Oona, quiet as always, watched her husband with a slight, tolerant smile while the rest of us roared with laughter.

The average number of guests at the Stewarts' on any Sunday was ten to fifteen, too many to record individually over the long period of our stay in England. One person, however, must be mentioned—Dr. W. E. B. Du Bois, a black American then in his nineties, but as active in mind and body as the average man of fifty. Although less well known to the American public than Malcolm X or Martin Luther King, Dr. Du Bois was the first of his people to organize the black movement in this country and to define its aspirations for advancement to full citizenship. He and his wife were on their way to Ghana as guests of its president when we met him; his mission there was to write a history of the black race from its earliest known origins to its present condition in both Africa and America. Perhaps it is inappropriate to apply the word *sexy* to a man of his age and stature, but I noticed that his eyes had an added twinkle when he gave his attention to some pretty young actresses who were among the guests. A few years later came the news of his death in Ghana, his massive work left for other scholars to complete.

Among the English friends we made in the course of our exile were Doris and Alexander Knox, both prominent in the London theatre and movies. Alex is best known in America for his fine portrayal of Wilson in the film by that name made by Darryl Zanuck at 20th Century–Fox. In recent years he has added several successful novels to his accomplishments. Moving from London, they converted an old Northumbrian castle on the sea into a comfortable home for themselves and their friends.

Another British couple with whom we have remained in contact over the years are Betty and Peter Lambda. Betty was a leading actress on the London stage and Peter a sculptor who had done portraits in bronze of such celebrities as Laurence Olivier, Vivien Leigh, and Aneurin Bevan, a former prime minister. Before we left England, he presented us with a bust of our son, Peter, at age nine, which now stands on our deck as a treasured reminder of our London years.

Many Americans regard the English as "stuffy," but in our experiences we found them open and friendly, from the Cockney bus and taxi drivers to members of Parliament. An extreme of informality was illustrated in an amusing incident that happened to the Lambdas. Peter had received a commission to sculpt the busts of the deposed king and queen of Siam (now Thailand), who lived on an estate in Cornwall. Never having had any traffic with kings, he and Betty bought some expensive clothes which they felt were appropriate for visiting royalty. When they arrived at the impressive manor house, the butler escorted them through the spacious halls outside to a formal garden, where they were presented to the king and his lovely queen—both stark naked.

After the first shock wave had passed over them, Peter and Betty rallied to acknowledge the greetings of the royal couple, who then introduced them to the other guests, mostly English, also without so much as a fig leaf. When the king suggested they disrobe to be in fashion with the others, this was something of an ordeal, but a monarch's request amounts to a command, so the Lambdas, standing behind a bush, removed their clothes, the butler taking charge of them. When they rejoined the group, who were in lively conversation, they were immediately included and soon they were as un-self-consc: ns as the others. However, in recounting the experience to us, Peter admitted that at first, since there were some very attractive female bodies in the gathering, including that of the queen, he had a little trouble keeping a certain interested member of his anatomy from rising to the royal occasion.

Several liberal members of Parliament took a special interest in their blacklisted American guests. We became well acquainted with Elwyn Jones, who had been chief English counsel in the Nuremburg trials and is now a member of the House of Lords. I can't quite imagine Elwyn being costumed and addressed as "Lord," since he was one of the most informal men we have ever met. Toward the end of our stay in England, we lived for several weeks in his home outside London. Always in a gay and jocular mood, he would entertain us with Welsh songs, Wales being his place of origin, while breakfast was being prepared. As a member of the government, Elwyn might have serious matters to deal with later in the day, but the early morning was a time for music and fun which we celebrated together. He was particularly fond of Anne, and when we left England, he came down to the boat train to see us off, presenting her with a bouquet of flowers indigenous to his native Wales. If only men like Elwyn Jones ran the governments of the world, there would be no more noise of guns and bombs—only music.

We had lived in England for four years. Having heard that McCarthyism was on the wane, we held a family conference. Peter was old enough to cast his vote, and the unanimous decision was to return home. England and the English had been very good to us, but America was our country, and Woodstock we had adopted as our hometown. Some of our friends, like the Browns, Joe Losey, and the Stewarts, had elected to live permanently in Europe; others were staying until they were certain they could return to work in whatever field had been closed to them. The *Queen Elizabeth* was our *Mayflower*, only this time leaving a friendly shore for one whose welcoming words are engraved on that lady holding a torch in New York harbor. Would she keep her promise this time?

RETURN

The year was 1956. By then the various "subversive" lists—black, pink, and gray—were fading with their chief exponent, McCarthy, in disgrace and out of power. However, there were still some holdover lists of "unemployables" kept by private organizations and individuals, such as the wholesale grocer in Syracuse.

As soon as we returned, my agent had a screenwriting assignment for me, but the producer discovered I was still on one of the lists influential enough to prevent my working in films. A friendly executive at United Artists arranged a meeting for me with Edward Bennett Williams, a prominent Washington attorney, who lately was given the honor of heading Nixon's infamous "enemies list." (Nixon was in the "list" business early in his career.)

Mr. Williams usually represented big-name clients. I was not so sanguine that he would handle my case, but to my surprise and delight, he readily agreed to represent me. I told him we were not rich, at the time an understatement, but it didn't bother him. He took a genuine interest in my problem, looked up my record (political and professional), and wrote my agent that I was "eminently employable" and to quote him to that effect.

Armed with this authoritative opinion, my agent made a second try. No change—I was still on the list. When I reported this to Mr. Williams, he picked up the phone, called the head of the organization blocking my employment, and wasted no words: "My client, Howard Koch, is off your list or we sue you for a million dollars. Take your choice."

I was off the list the next day.

Again free to work under my own name, I wrote a screenplay for Victor Saville at Columbia Pictures entitled *Greengage Summer*, based on a charming story by Rumer Godden (retitled in this country, for some reason best known to the distributor, *Loss of Innocence*). Saville had a record of distinguished pictures in both America and England. An ideal producer from a writer's standpoint, he let me dramatize the story without any interference beyond helpful suggestions. It dealt with the problems faced by three English children, ages ten to sixteen, left to their own resources in a French provincial hotel by a sick mother. The children, especially the oldest one, become involved in the intrigues of the adults to whom they have been entrusted. After some misadventures they come out of their experience wiser in the ways of the world, the oldest one, a girl, crossing the threshold of adolescence.

Casting a picture with children can be hazardous—they can easily become unbearably "cute"; but Victor found three, a boy and two girls, who were naturals for the roles. The adult leads were played by Kenneth More and Danielle Darrieux, both accomplished performers. The picture was shot mostly in the champagne country of France, beautifully photographed in the pastel tones of that countryside. The finished film received glowing notices in both New York and London and is often revived in theatres and on television. It also established a new young star— Susannah York.

Unlike many producers today who simply put together the "package" and then turn the production over to the director, Victor stayed with it throughout to be certain that the story values reached the screen. When the director wanted to make a change, Victor would call me on the transatlantic phone for my approval and rewrites. It gave me as much control over the script as though I had been on the set instead of three thousand miles away; Victor and I have kept up our friendship over the years.

This experience would be very rare today when most directors are given autonomous authority over the content of a film, even to the extent of rewriting scenes or improvising them on the set. In its contract negotiations the Writers Guild has succeeded in gaining benefits, mostly of a financial nature, for its membership, but the Guild has not yet felt strong enough to confront the industry on the central issue—some measure of control by the screenwriter over the story and characters he has created, the kind of protection afforded by the Dramatists Guild.

This is not to imply that a screenwriter, if given more control, will invariably create a masterpiece or even a satisfying film. That depends on his material, his talent, and his associates, including, of course, the director, who may add to or subtract from what he has put on paper. My next assignment was an example in point.

Arthur Hornblow, a well-established producer at Columbia, asked me to dramatize John Hersey's novel *The War Lover* for Columbia-British, where the film about American fliers stationed in England during World War II was to be made. For the leading role Hornblow wanted and needed Steve McQueen, then on his way up to becoming a superstar.

McQueen was interested in the part but insisted on conferring with the writer before he signed the contract. At the time he was making a low-budget war picture on location in the Sacramento Valley in northern California. Arthur asked me to go up there for a talk with Steve, as he wanted to close the deal and start pre-production preparations.

My son Hardy, then a graduate student at Stanford, and his wife wanted to drive up with me to watch some of the shooting and, of course, to meet Steve McQueen. It was summer and the temperature in the Sacramento Valley was around 110 with little change at night. The actors, wearing heavy army clothes, were trying to act as though they were in cool Normandy and the result was torture and flaring tempers.

We were Steve's guests at dinner that evening and he was the soul of charm. We talked a little about *The War Lover* but not in a serious enough way to justify the trip; Steve seemed satisfied and he assured me he would sign the contract to do the picture.

The next day we watched the shooting out on the parched field under a blazing sun. The actors were doing their best to cope with the trying conditions but progress was slow in getting the scene the way the director—and Steve—wanted it. Suddenly three men appeared, studio employees sent by the executive producer of the company financing the picture. The production was way over budget, a cardinal sin in the movie world, and the men had orders to seize the cameras, which would shut down the location shooting. Whatever remained to be photographed would be done back at the studio under the watchful eye of the producer.

It was then that we had an insight into a side of Steve's personality that brooked no interference with whatever he wanted to do, whether it was to drive his car eighty miles an hour through city streets or to start a fight. The three cameras were clustered about twenty feet away. Steve walked over, picked up a stick, and drew a circle in the sand around the cameras. Then he faced the three intruders, pointing to the line he had drawn.

"Anyone steps over that line gets the shit knocked out of him."

The three men decided retreat was the better part of valor; the company finished the shooting on location.

Later I joined Arthur Hornblow in London for consultation and rewrites. Steve arrived soon after. From our first encounter I knew

I would have an assertive actor to deal with in any problem affecting the part he was to play. Steve was also addicted to racing cars and motorcycles, both on the restricted list of the company insuring the production. He paid no attention.

One day in his Knightsbridge apartment we came into sharp conflict on a change he demanded in the screenplay. We managed to work out an acceptable compromise, but I warned Steve that Arthur Hornblow would have to approve the change. He summarily dismissed this reservation.

"The hell with whether he approves or not."

"But, Steve, he's the producer."

"So what? He needs me more than I need him."

Steve was speaking the truth. If the star quits a picture costing several million dollars, the financing will be withdrawn, and the preproduction money already spent will be lost. Arthur and the director, Stephen Leacock, took the change with good grace and the film was made. Despite our differences, I came to like Steve, and by the end of the shooting we had become friends.

As for the picture, it probably made back its cost and possibly some profit, but to me it was a failure for which I held myself accountable. Out of my respect for Hersey I had adhered too closely to the novel, which had more characters and situations than could be compressed into a two-hour film. As a result the motivations were not fully realized; the characterizations lacked the depth to make them credible. I should have hewed to a simpler dramatic line, leaving room for the revealing details that would flesh out the characters. The technical effects relating to the vintage planes and their bombing missions were well done. Aside from this, whatever interest the film held came, not from the story, but from Steve's personality projected on the screen. A writer doesn't always need another more dominant associate—director, producer, star, or whatever—to wreck a film. Taking the wrong approach to the material, he can do it all by himself.

While I was working on *The War Lover*, Anne read *The Fox* by D. H. Lawrence and thought it would make an interesting film.

I agreed with her, and we bought the movie rights from the
Lawrence estate and then went to Victor Saville to enlist him in
plans for its production.

Victor saw the story's possibilities. He agreed to produce and
I went to work on the screenplay. Since the novella had only three
characters and a fox, I had to find ways to extend the story without violating Lawrence's characterizations and the foreboding
mood he had created. When the script was finished, the casting
quickly fell into place. Vivien Leigh and Patricia Neal agreed to
play the two women who had taken refuge from the world on a
small, isolated farm in the Midlands where they were harassed by
a marauding fox preying on their chickens.

In Lawrence's imagery the fox represented the male element
missing in the lives of the two women. For the young man who,
foxlike, enters their lives as a disruptive influence we had a verbal
commitment from Alan Bates, now a reigning film star, then a
talented stage actor just right in age and personality for the role.
I had begun conferences with John Schlesinger, who was interested in directing.

From its inception the project seemed well starred in both
senses. But before production could be set up, Saville became
seriously ill and was hospitalized for most of a year, leaving us
without a producer. At the same time Patricia Neal became
pregnant, misnamed an act of God from our point of view. Begun so auspiciously, the project completely disintegrated.

We returned to America, still determined to put *The Fox* on
the screen. My agent tried all the major studios, but it was turned
down on the grounds that it was an "art picture" and therefore
not box office. Then one evening at a dinner party at my agent's
home in Bel Air, I happened to be seated next to an attractive
English actress, Anne Heywood, who had just played the lead in
a small European film. She and her husband, Raymond Stross,
were looking for a literary property that would launch her movie
career in this country. She asked me if I had a story with a strong
female role within her age range. She was in her middle twenties,

somewhat younger than I had envisioned for the part, but she had a dormant quality that might be right for one of the two women. When I told her briefly the story of *The Fox*, she became interested and asked me to send her my script to the Château Marmont where they were staying.

They read the screenplay immediately; the next day I had an urgent message to call them at the Château. They were both excited. They *had* to do the picture. It was exactly the kind of role she had been looking for. Would I sell them an option? They would pay me an advance and a substantial percentage in the profits of the picture. *And* they wanted *no* changes, not a word. They could even put a clause in our contract giving me complete control of my script. As far as they were concerned, it was ready to go.

I liked Anne Heywood but I was less impressed by Stross, who would produce. He was obviously more a promoter than an experienced filmmaker, and as far as I could see the only thing he had to promote was his wife. However, the story had been rejected by so many producers that I decided to take the chance. As it turned out, I had reason to regret my choice.

After considerable scrambling, giving away bits and pieces of the picture, Stross raised enough money to finance the production with a Warner distribution guarantee. For the other woman he signed Sandy Dennis, a capable actress with some strange mannerisms that might fit this particular role but, again, younger than I had considered ideal for the part. For the male role he cast Keir Dullea, a good actor, but without the foxlike quality Alan Bates would have suggested. Since there was a tight budget of a million dollars, low for a major film, Stross engaged a young director, Mark Rydell, who was not well known at the time.

When Rydell appeared at our place in Woodstock, he had a list of changes he wanted me to make in the script. They were minor revisions and I accepted most of them. Later Stross called me from Hollywood. This time he was asking for what I considered a major change. In the original story Lawrence had left the relationship between the two women ambivalent, letting the audience read into it whatever they liked. This I was careful to preserve. Now Stross was demanding a scene to be written which would establish an overt lesbian relationship. And the mystic quality of the affair between the "fox" (Dullea) and Heywood would be conventionalized into another "wrestling in the hay" scene.

I objected strenuously, reminding Stross of his promise not to change a word without my approval. My arguments failed to move him. In a heated conversation he warned me he would put on another writer if I refused to do the scene. I appealed to the Writers Guild for protection under the clause in my contract; if they had been willing to place Stross on their "unfair list," no other writer would have been allowed to work for him. I pointed out that the clause giving me control over my work would be a breakthrough for screenwriters, who are ordinarily at the mercy of the producer and director. For whatever reason, the Guild chose not to intercede. Since the clause was legally binding, I could have gone to court to enjoin the production, but this would have accomplished nothing but putting *The Fox* into legal limbo.

Another writer was hired to make the changes I had rejected. The picture was made and became a box-office success, grossing ten times its cost. Even the reviews were favorable except for Pauline Kael in *The New Yorker*, who had read the Lawrence story and knew what had been lost in transposing it to the screen. The ambivalent relationship had been made obvious and the poetic imagery sacrificed for sensationalism. Since I owned a percentage, we profited in money terms, but hardly in satisfaction. There is a vast difference between a successful picture and one whose high potential is fully realized.

Aside from my professional interest, I go to the movies to live vicariously in the two-hour world a storyteller has created. However, it is becoming increasingly difficult to find films made today with whose characters I can identify. Often they seem more like illustrations of a story than the story itself. They can impress us with their photographic beauty, titillate us with their sensuality, and shock us with their creepy horrors, but rarely do they enlist our feelings. In so many areas of modern life we have become spectators, whether it is a political event we are watching, a football game, or a movie. In neither the real nor the fictional world are we asked to participate. The images flash across our screens and we look at them from an emotional distance. The eye is sated, the glands stimulated, but the heart is left hungry.

In the past several years three stories were offered me to dramatize for the screen. Two were Cold War spy stories; one was set in the Civil War period in the vein of *Gone with the Wind*. None had the slightest interest for me and I have returned to the theatre where I began. One play is under option for Broadway; another is going the rounds. Nothing is ever certain in the theatre, but the chance to write what you want is worth the hazards.

In John Houseman's introduction, identifying my philosophy with that of Candide, I have to point out an important distinction. I do not believe this is "the best of all possible worlds." Far from it. This is the world we inherited from some of the darker pages of history and we have not yet turned the page. The jungle values—predatory, possessive, territorially minded—still prevail in ruling circles the world over. Can these be transformed to ones that support our common humanity and the small, fragile earth which we share? Who can say with any certainty? To quote a line from one of Bob Dylan's lyrics, "The answer, my friend, is blowing in the wind." However, I see some signs of change in the consciousness of individuals, particularly but not exclusively in that of the young, possible forerunners of a new, humanist-oriented value system. As our world teeters between nuclear war and ecological disaster, the stake is now survival—nothing less—and I place my chips and my hopes on the future. Houseman is right. I *am* an optimist.

And what of our private world? I sit here on the deck of our home penciling these notes and looking down at a clear mountain-bred stream with a tall wood of pine and hemlock on the opposite bank. Three previous parts of my life have drifted through time as the current of that stream presses toward the ocean, where it will find renewal in some other form.

Anne and I have crossed out the option clauses in our marriage contract and have marked it "in perpetuity." Our family and friends are as close to us as thought and feeling can bring them. Our children, now adults, have four children of their own, three girls and a boy, free in spirit and more mature than I was at twice their age. Multiplied by millions, they may be among the fore-runners of what I term the "new people," those on whom human survival may depend. Far from rich, we all live comfortably, even with some luxuries, more fortunate than most, the result of chance as much as choice.

Woodstock suits our temperaments better than any of our various former homes. Founded as an art colony by two utopians, Hervey White and Ralph Whitehead, it still carries on their tradition of creativity. Painters, writers, musicians, craftsmen, publishers, naturalists, doctors, actors, lawyers, businessmen, adventurers—all somehow blend into a community. Its life-style offers the basic freedom to live as one chooses and to respect the same right in others. The local newspaper serves as a forum for all viewpoints from far left to far right to far out.

An elderly archbishop of the Greek Orthodox faith, known locally and affectionately as the "hippie priest," has come to Woodstock, where he has chosen as his "cathedral" a small mountainside chapel. The young flock to him with their troubles and their celebrations, a songfest or a wedding. A stone's throw away is an old hotel converted into a Buddhist temple—no stones are thrown. An amateur astronomer gazes at the same stars as his astrologist neighbor. One charts their course; the other reads their signs—no stars are crossed. In the town hall meetings Woodstockers debate the desirability of a new sewerage system with as much heat as though they were settling the affairs of nations—but no blood is shed.

So nonconformist is the ambience of Woodstock that not even the weather vanes agree on the direction of the wind. Many times I have watched the vane on the Dutch church point east when the one on the town hall insisted on pointing west. But who cares which way the wind blows so long as it refreshes a way of life that draws creative people from all parts of the world? There is a saying that many have come to Woodstock for a weekend and stayed for the rest of their lives.

To the young, Woodstock is Hamelin Town, its music from folk to rock to classical pouring out of homes and studios and playing the role of the Pied Piper. Our grandson, Jamie, age ten, has been caught by its siren song, following in the wake of many others. We have a small pedal boat on our stream, used for crossing to the wooded paths on the other side. Jamie, when visiting here, would ferry us over and receive a nickel fare for the voyage. A short time ago a great tree fell across the stream fifty yards below our house. Jamie converted it into a bridge and, being ecologically minded, he brought in nothing that was not natural to the environment. Cutting branches from the fallen tree, he fashioned them into a handrail to make the crossing safe. That evening I went down to see the finished product. On the path close to the bridge was a sign he had painted on a board and nailed to a tree: TOLL FREE. ENJOY THE CROSSING.

Jamie, the ferryman, was doing himself out of the ferry business, but he opted for another value. I stood there thinking of what a world it could be if signs went up on all the paths we take to our various destinations. Toll free. Enjoy the crossing.